About Master Limited Pai

In a low yield world where government bonds pay next to no interest, S&P 500 stocks pay little more than that in dividends, the Canadian government is on the threshold of taxing income trusts, and even real estate investment trusts are suffering cash flow problems, one type of security still stands as a beacon of hope to income investors.

Master Limited Partnerships — MLPs

Until now, the information available to investors has been scanty. There've been only chapters in books. One prominent financial advice company recently launched a newsletter devoted to them, but the price tag is $399 annually. The Internet contains summary but incomplete articles and snatches of advice (some good, some inaccurate).

Finally, investors can learn all about these terrific investments — their rewards and risks; the paperwork hassles and how to get around them; and how to invest in them using both taxable and tax-deferred accounts —

In one convenient volume for one low price. This book is the first and only.

You'll discover:

The incredible benefits of Master Limited Partnerships

Why they're still incredibly cheap

How their legal rules and business structure combine to send you lots of cash

Why they'll continue to generate lots of cash for the foreseeable future

Information on every company

Information on every MLP index

Information on every MLP closed-end fund

What MLP i-units are and how they can skyrocket your IRA portfolio

How to understand and complete MLP tax forms

Everything you need to know to get started to enhance your current income or save for your financially secure future.

Praise for Richard Stooker's Previous Book INCOME INVESTING SECRETS

"Rick Stooker is on the right track. We also intend to pursue a more income-oriented strategy in the years to come. Capital gains are subject to both the risk of a decline in economic fundamentals and a deterioration in market psychology. High-quality dividends and income are subject only to the former, and that makes a big difference in modeling your portfolio returns in retirement."

— *Charles Lewis Sizemore CFA, Senior Analyst HS Dent Investment Management, LLC http://www.hsdent.com/*

"I am a Chartered Accountant in Canada and spent most of my career teaching in a community college.

"Over the years, I have used various "plans," with varying degrees of success, but had never given much thought to dividends, so I fell prey to the hype about capital gains. So what was I thinking? Should have been investing for dividends.

"I also learned about some new investment vehicles, and got a "heads up" on some investments that I was aware of, but put on the back burner.

"Wish I knew about all this stuff when I was in my 20's, or at least paid attention to the theories involved in my 40's."

—- *Dennis Wilson*

"What an eye-opener!!!

"I had heard about REITs, MLPs, BDCs, but you really explained their advantages and disadvantages. Thank you, Rick. You have set me on the right path to generate a steady income stream."

— *Kenny H*

While the financial markets are collapsing . . .

Finally, you too can discover the old-fashioned — yet now revolutionary (and updated for the 21st century) —"gold egg" income investing secrets for lazy investors

Master Limited Partnerships

High-Yield, Ever-Growing Oil "Stocks" Income Investing for a Secure, Worry-Free and Comfortable Retirement

by Richard Stooker

Published by Info Ring Press

ISBN: 1451534140

EAN-13: 9781451534146

DISCLAIMER

I am not a broker.

I am not a licensed securities dealer or representative of any kind.

I am no legal right to sell you securities and I'm not trying to do so.

Nothing in this book is to be construed as a solicitation or offer to sell you securities.

Nothing in this book is to be construed as personal financial advice.

I have no legal right to give you personal financial advice. Even if I was a registered financial adviser, which I'm not, I don't know you or your individual financial situation.

This book is the result of my research and is believed accurate. It consists of my opinions and suggestions.

I'm not making any representations as to how much money you will make if you invest according to the guidelines I set forth —that will depend upon the payouts of dividends and interest of the precise securities you decide to invest in, and nobody can predict the future.

That is part of the problem with mainstream financial advice — it assumes the future will repeat the past. It doesn't.

Past performance is not indicative of future results.

This book is for education and entertainment. Nothing in this book is to be construed as professional advice. For that, you should consult your attorney, accountant or financial adviser.

I am not responsible for the results of your investment decisions.

You must read, think over what I say, make your own investment decisions and take responsibility for your own life, including the results of your investment decisions.

Continuing to read this book implies your acceptance of these terms.

LEGAL NOTICE

Full Disclosure

In the field of investment writing there can be a suspicion the author is practicing some form of "front running."

That is, promoting a particular security that the writer has already bought, so more people will buy it, driving up the price and therefore giving the writer the chance to sell their shares at a big profit.

Some advice newsletter companies and writers have been accused of this kind of "pump and dump" or "short and distort" activity. And it certainly takes place in Internet investing chat rooms and via spam.

I believe some companies such as BARRON'S do not allow their staffers to buy shares in companies they write about, to avoid even the appearance of impropriety. BARRON'S has enough readers and clout to drive market prices up or down.

Nobody has paid me to write this book. I wrote it because I'm interested in all types of income-producing investments, and there are no other books devoted to Master Limited Partnerships. Therefore, it was an unfilled niche.

My own investing philosophy is to continue to buy income producing investments and then reinvest the proceeds. And hold forever.

Therefore — and I know this is a novel concept, but it's logical — I'm better off if the price of my securities remains as low as possible. The lower their market prices, the more shares or units I can buy when I buy more shares or units and when I reinvest the income from my portfolio.

Therefore, it would be better for my personal portfolio to keep the market price of Master Limited Partnerships as low as possible.

But I also have a professional obligation as an author to bring you the best information possible.

And besides, I have no expectation that this book will sell enough copies (it's not in the same league as BARRON'S!) to influence the market price of any MLP.

I do plan to continue to buy MLP units and related investments, along with other income-generating investments such as the ones I describe in my other book Income Investing Secrets, for my own accounts for the rest of my life.

I'm writing about Master Limited Partnerships for the same reason I'm investing in them — because I believe that, as a group, they're the best and safest income investments available.

Table of Contents

Introduction

I wrote this book because nobody else did.

You can buy books about Real Estate Investment Trusts (REIT), Canadian income trusts, ordinary dividend paying stocks, bonds and utility stocks. You can buy books that have a chapter or appendix about Master Limited Partnerships.

But — until now — you could not buy a book devoted solely to Master Limited Partnerships.

I cover a lot of material that applies to all energy-related MLPs, but my strong recommendation is that you confine your investment dollars to those in what are called "midstream" MLPs. More on that later.

I'll start off with a chapter that explains the many benefits of investing in midstream Master Limited Partnerships.

Followed by a chapter on the "catches" — the aspects that individual investors sometimes stumble over.

Followed by information on the business risks of MLPs.

Then information on their history, structure and businesses both from the financial side and the petroleum industry side. This includes why businesses convert their assets to MLPs. And why such high yielding investments are still available in today's otherwise low-yield financial marketplace.

Then we'll cover everybody's favorite topic — taxes. The tax and tax filing consequences of owning MLP units. I'll also cover the various tax forms and how to complete them.

Then ways of investing in MLPs that, in terms of tax paperwork and filing, are the same as investing in stocks. So you can add MLPs to your tax-deferred accounts or simply avoid the extra paperwork created by direct ownership of MLP units.

How to Invest in MLPs — All Aspects

There're chapters on MLP i-units, on each MLP-related closed-end fund and MLP Exchange Traded Notes.

Then there're chapters on all the MLP indexes.

Then tips on putting this information all together to benefit from MLPs in your taxable broker account and your tax-deferred accounts.

And how to balance MLPs with the rest of your portfolio.

Then a chapter on what happens if you — against my advice — sell MLP units.

And a chapter on what happens if you follow my advice and hold your MLP units until you die.

Then chapters on each individual energy or natural resource-related MLP available today.

If there are any omissions or errors I need to correct in a future edition, email me at — rick@inforingpress.com .

Chapter 1

Why You're Going to Love Master Limited Partnerships

Before we get into a lot of detail, let me explain up front the bottom line —

Smart Investors Should Love Master Limited Partnerships

There's a lot of reasons for that, and I hope you'll read the best of this book so you understand I'm not speaking off the top of head and so you understand and believe what I'm saying.

But I want you to know — from the get-go — why reading this book (and of course, actually acting on this information) will make you money.

Lots of money.

Master Limited Partnerships—

1. Pay out large amounts of cash on a quarterly basis.

This varies, but it's not unusual to find MLPs yielding an average of seven or eight percent.

If you buy an S&P 500 index fund, you'll receive a 1.78% yield (as I write these words in February 2010). If you count only the S&P 500 stocks that actually pay a dividend, you'll still receive only a 2.42% yield.

And that in a stock market which is still below the level it first hit in April 1999.

2. For about the first five years that you own units of an MLP, roughly 80% of that cash is NOT taxable until and unless you sell it. If you never sell, you never pay taxes on it.

3. That quarterly cash generally goes up every year. That's not guaranteed or universal of course, but the historical average is around 9% annual growth.

2008 and 2009 were hard on some MLPs, but not as hard as they were on the rest of the world's financial markets.

4. Over the past fifteen years, according to one of the MLP indexes, the types of MLPs this book concentrates on have gone up in market price 550%. That's an average compound total annual return of 14.5%.

The S&P 500 went up 120%, or just 5.6% annually.

Those are averages, but the only period that MLPs as a whole did not go up in price more than the general stock market was 1998-1999, the height of the dot com high tech boom.

For the twelve-month period ending October 31, 2009 (one of the most unnerving periods in the history of the financial markets), MLPs posted a gain of 24.22% while the S&P 500 went up just 9.80%.

And remember — the broad stock market is right now still about where it was in April 1999.

5. The amount of cash paid quarterly has one-third the volatility of the S&P 500 stock dividends.

That means your cash income from MLPs is three times as likely to remain high or higher than dividends from average S&P 500 stocks — which can be cut. During the current recession, many were.

6. Market performance does not correlate strongly with the stock market.

This means that MLP share prices can rise even while the S&P 500 market is going down. Therefore, owning MLPs can act as a hedge on your portfolio.

I must point out, however, that this is historically true in the long run, BUT in the financial crisis of 2008 through March 2009 ALL securities suffered, MLPs included (but not as much as most types of investments).

7. Are in a business with high and relatively inelastic demand — energy.

Energy demand does fluctuate, and during the 2002 and current recessions, it remained flat — but not down.

8. Are in a business with growing demand.

Experts believe that American demand for energy will continue to grow at least 1% per year for the next twenty years.

9. Do not depend on a high price for gas on oil.

During slow economic periods, the price for oil goes down. But that doesn't affect MLPs. Unlike oil companies, MLPs I recommend in this book make a profit whether oil is selling for $10 per barrel or $150.

10. Prices are set by regulators who guarantee they make a profit.

Pipeline MLPs are regulated by the Federal Energy Regulatory Commission (FERC). They're guaranteed a profit, much like utilities. However, unlike utilities, they're not required to share cuts in expenses with their customers.

This means that a good management team has an incentive to cut costs as much as possible — which means more money for you.

11. If and when society transitions to using alternative, non-petroleum based sources of energy, many MLPs can be converted to ethanol and hydrogen.

Mmm, Let's See . . .

An investment that pays out a quarterly cash yield about four times the S&P 500 average, and that is largely tax deferred until you sell the security (which means taxes can be forever deferred), and that distribution grows an average of 9% annually, and that security price goes up faster than the S&P 500 average even when the S&P 500 falls, and which is in a business necessary to civilization as we know it, with price protection enforced by the government, and with a future all but assured . . .

If you're not excited yet, you need to check your pulse or you're so rich already you're bored by money.

So by now you're probably like the people in some radio ads, asking, "What's the catch?"

Chapter 2

The "Catches" of Investing in Master Limited Partnerships

There are four.

1. MLPs are NOT for tax-deferred accounts.

Frankly, if your entire investment portfolio is a tax-deferred account, direct ownership of Master Limited Partnerships are not — yet — for you. But there are ways to benefit from their extraordinary cash flow. I cover these in later chapters.

2. In February or March of every year, you receive a partnership tax form K-1 instead of an ordinary 1099-DIV in January.

K-1 forms are a lot more complicated and confusing than ordinary 1099-DIV forms.

And they require that you keep good records, which you should do anyway.

That's why there's a chapter on them in this book. If you do your own taxes, you'll learn what you need.

Plus, any competent accountant knows how to use a K-1 form to prepare your tax return. So if you don't do your own taxes, you don't have to sweat about it all.

And almost all MLPs use an online service to export your K-1 information to Turbo Tax.

3. With some MLPs, you're legally supposed to report your earnings to every state in which the MLP does business.

4. If you are foolish enough to sell your MLP units, your original tax basis amount is taxed as ordinary income.

You can avoid this catch, simply by never selling your MLP units. That's my advice.

Maybe you're thinking that there must be another catch, something else I'm not telling you.

I don't blame you for not believing all the above benefits. They sound too good to be true.

That's the purpose of the remainder of this book — to explain Master Limited Partnerships in detail, so you understand the technical, legal and practical reasons why they're such great investments.

They seem like perfect businesses to invest it, but there're always risks.

Chapter 3

The Risks Master Limited Partnerships Face

1. Business risk

Some management teams simply perform better than others.

2. Regulatory risk

There's always the possibility that Congress could someday change the regulatory structure, law, regulations or practices of the Federal Energy Regulatory Commission (FERC) to something less favorable to MLPs.

That does not appear likely right now, but nobody can predict the future.

Their trade group, the National Association of Publicly Traded Partnerships, will fight any such proposal.

3. Terrorism

Some parts of the energy processing system are natural targets.

Pipelines can run for thousands of miles however, so the risk of damage to them is limited. Refineries, oil wells and other areas with a large concentration of equipment are more vulnerable.

Master Limited Partnerships are highly conscious of security. And they buy insurance against terrorism.

4. Weather

In the fall of 2005 we saw how the damage Hurricane Katrina did to the Gulf Coast oil industry drastically affected gas prices.

Some MLPs, such as natural gas and propane, can be adversely affected by warm weather in the winter, because that reduces demand from people heating their homes.

5. Cap and Trade

This is a proposal for the government to set a limit on the amount of carbon dioxide (CO2) that the country could release into the atmosphere. Companies could buy and sell permits to release CO2. Over time, the amount of CO2 allowed would go down.

Industries that release a lot of CO2, such as those that rely on burning oil, natural gas and coal, would eventually have to pay a lot of money for the permits. Those costs would be passed on to consumers, amounting to huge price increases for goods and services.

In effect, the federal government would be claiming the right — new in law — to control the amount of CO2 released into the atmosphere. And it would charge companies for releasing CO2 into the atmosphere.

Because burning carbon fuel has never before been regulated, this would be in effect a massive new federal tax — which is why its critics often refer to it as "Cap and Tax."

Any extra taxes on energy usage would adversely affect MLPs.

6. Interest rates

There's a misconception that MLPs are a sort of fixed-income security such as a bond. And therefore, when interest rates go up, the price of MLPs goes down.

That is not correct. MLPs are not like bonds at all. However, higher interest rates do mean a higher cost of capital for MLPs, and therefore reduce their profits.

This is true of all businesses. Higher interest rates make it harder and more expensive to borrow money.

7. Economic downturns

The effect of recessions on MLPs is limited, because demand for energy is considered "inelastic." And many MLPs have contracts which require a certain volume of business from their customers.

However, in a drastic scenario, if energy prices go up a lot or Americans are otherwise faced with hard times, they would cut back on energy usage. That would reduce demand for oil and natural gas.

8. Legislative

It's conceivable that Congress could pass a law rescinding the tax-exempt status of MLPs.

It does not appear likely, but we cannot predict the future.

Their trade group, the National Association of Publicly Traded Partnerships, will fight any such proposal.

9. Environmental liability damage

No MLP wants to cause an Exxon/Valdez type of tragedy, but anything in life is possible.

All MLPs carry a lot of insurance against environmental problems.

10. Supplies of energy to transport

Every pipeline needs something to transport. If there's a disruption of oil or natural gas supply, that can be a problem.

This could be caused by a disruption affecting imported forms of energy. For example, a war in the Middle East.

It could also be caused by one customer going bankrupt or taking their business to another pipeline.

11. Equity Crisis

MLPs depend on ready access to capital, especially because they're required to distribute their cash to unit holders.

During a liquidity crisis such as 2008-2009, access to capital is a lot more difficult and more expensive.

12. Legal problems

Any person or company with cash can become a target for lawsuits. MLPs are no exception.

13. Exposure to energy price fluctuations

There's a misconception that Master Limited Partnerships are a way to invest in "commodities."

In general, especially for the "midstream" MLPs that this book recommends, that is not true. Pipeline MLPs make money by transporting crude oil, refined petroleum products and natural gas based on volume, NOT their cost.

However, some MLPs are involved to some degree in other parts of the energy business process. They can be hurt when energy prices are low.

Midstream MLPs can be hurt to a degree when energy prices are so high than they discourage consumption — and therefore their volume of business is reduced.

14. Extreme technological change

What if someone invents a cheap and easy way for everyone to use solar, wind or water power for everything we need from running our cars to powering our computers?

There'd be no need for carbon-based energy products.

However, nobody believes this is more than an extreme, green utopian vision — at least for now.

Master Limited Partnerships are real world businesses. They face real world problems. For investors, they have many advantages.

The real world comes with problems.

However, MLPs deal with them as well as possible.

And all other businesses face many of the same risks. For instance, when interest rates go up, all businesses are affected. Therefore, there's no way for a stock market investor to "escape" that risk.

(You could buy bonds, but then you're exposed to the investment risk of owning bonds.)

Master Limited Partnerships Have One Major Advantage Over All Other Businesses — Everything Else Relies on Them

Energy is the most basic, fundamental need of human beings and our civilization.

You can freeze to death faster than you can starve to death.

And food depends on fertilizer, which uses energy.

Besides, while "food" in some form is a basic need, consumers can choose whether or not to buy chicken or spaghetti or go out to McDonald's.

11

You have many fewer choices about the forms of energy you must use in your daily life.

Let's see. You can now choose to drive a hybrid or an all-gasoline car. To buy Regular or Premium gasoline. To cook with gas or electricity. Or to put a windmill in your backyard or solar panels on your roof.

That's about it.

For the foreseeable future, until we build a totally green society based on local, renewable energy or descend back into primitive barbarity, we need the forms of energy that Master Limited Partnerships deliver to us.

But just what is a Master Limited Partnership?

Let's start by examining what is a limited partnership.

Chapter 4

What's a Limited Partnership

A Master Limited Partnership is a special form of limited partnership.

So, to understand them, it helps to understand what a limited partnership is.

And to understand limited partnerships, let's start with partnerships.

You and Joe Start a Pizzeria

Let's say that you and your buddy Joe have a great idea for a pizzeria. You work together, you both put in some money, you both work long and hard to make the business successful.

You and Joe are partners.

You own the business together. You both invested your time, sweat and money. At the end of every month when your accountant figures out your profits, you and Joe split them fifty-fifty.

You don't think about it much, but you and Joe are also splitting the risk — only that split is not fifty-fifty, it's more like one hundred-one hundred.

How can that be? You both are fully liable for the business debts and problems of the business.

One day Joe mixes up a batch of bad pizza dough, and it turns the customers' hair green. They find a good class action lawyer and sue you and Joe for one million dollars.

You get a lawyer too but, what you can do? — the customers have green hair, so you lose the case. You and Joe sell the pizza oven on eBay and give them that money, but it's a far cry from one million dollars.

With the pizzeria closed, their customers' lawyer goes after you and Joe personally.

Turns out that Joe has no money. You, however, have a nice house and some stocks in your brokerage account.

When the opposing lawyer comes to collect the million dollar court settlement, they get nothing from Joe, but take your house and your stock — all one million dollars.

Yes, although you were not responsible for turning the customers' hair green and although you received only half the profits of the business, you're responsible for one hundred percent of its debts and liabilities. Just because they couldn't get any money out of Joe.

You and Joe are Pizza Partners Again

Now let's say that your buddy Joe is the only one who wants or knows how to run a pizzeria. You don't have the time or expertise.

But you've got the money it'll take to buy an oven, cheese and sauce, rent out a location, hire some employees, and advertise on the radio.

Joe makes you an offer. You put up the money. He does all the work. At the end of the month, you still split the profits fifty-fifty.

You know Joe and you're sure he knows a lot about running pizzerias. You also believe he's honest and competent and you trust him.

So maybe you figure that's a good deal. Joe works eighty hours a week in the business. You work zero hours. But you receive half the profits.

Besides, you figure that if the business goes under, you can also sell the pizza oven on eBay and make back half your money.

(In the real world, the details could change. Depending on how well you and Joe know and trust each other, and how desperate he is for the start up capital you might receive ten percent or net profits or ninety percent.)

(Also, many times the partner with the money is a seasoned, successful business person. They don't work the business, but they give advice that helps the business succeed, not just money.)

Again, all goes well for a while — and then Joe mixes that batch of bad pizza dough and the customers' hair turns green and you again wind up paying the entire million dollars.

Ordinary Partnerships Are Risky Forms of Business

This is why any business adviser worth their salt will tell you to be extremely careful who you go into business with. In an ordinary partnership, the partners split profits fifty-fifty but are each responsible for one hundred percent of the debts.

It's not unusual for one person to abandon the business, sticking the other partner with all the debts.

Limited Partnerships Limit the Risk

Now, let's say that Joe is still trying to raise the money to start up his pizzeria and he approaches you.

He needs more money than you can pay by yourself. But you have nine good friends who'd like the chance to invest in a pizzeria and share in the profits while Joe spends eighty hours a week topping pizzas with pepperoni in front of a five hundred fifty degree pizza oven.

The nine of you agree to each put in the same amount of money and to share equally in the profits.

As the worker, Joe will get fifty percent of the net profits.

The ten financial backers will each get one-tenth of the remaining fifty percent, or 5% each.

However, the ten of you are street smart. You've been burned before. You trust Joe, but you still want to make sure you'll never be ripped off again.

Therefore, you go to a lawyer who draws up an official partnership agreement that you all sign off on.

You ten financial backers agree to put in the required money. (Let's say $10,000 each.) In return, you agree to accept 5% of net profits every month.

You also agree that you will not try to run the business for Joe.

Joe agrees to run the business. He will not put in any money, but he is one hundred percent responsible for hiring, firing, making pizzas, delivering pizzas and so on.

He also agrees that the ten of you are not responsible for putting in any money other than the original $10,000.

This is a limited partnership.

You and your nine friends play a significant but limited role — you put in $10,000 each.

You do no work.

You have no other risk.

When Joe mixes up that bad batch of dough and turns the customers' hair green, what happens?

The business closes. Joe sells the pizza oven on eBay and turns over that money to the customers' attorney.

The attorney goes after Joe. Because Joe has nothing more to pay, the customers and their lawyer wind up with only the money from selling the pizza oven.

You and your friends have lost your $10,000 investment. You're not happy about that. But nobody sues you or your friends for your personal money.

Why not?

Limited Partners in a Limited Partnership are Responsible Only for the Money They Invest in the Business

Your liability is limited by the terms of the partnership. Yes, you do lose the $10,000 you invested in Joe's Pizzeria — but that's it. You keep your house, your bank account, your stocks, and everything else.

The other lawyer has no legal recourse against you.

So you're safe.

In this case, Joe was the partnership's General Partner.

You and your nine friends were the partnership's Limited Partners.

The General Partner runs the business.

The Limited Partners put up the funds but generally have nothing to say about running the business. That's the job of the GP.

And Limited Partners have limited risk — it's limited to the amount of money they invest. They can lose that, but nothing else.

A lot of businesses are Limited Partnerships. As you can see, they make a lot of sense.

Now, as I Mentioned, a Master Limited Partnership is a Special Kind of Limited Partnership

Let's say that after a few years of being a Limited Partner behind Joe's Pizzeria, you decide you'd like to sell your share of the partnership and move to Florida. You enjoy the monthly income, but you need a lot of cash to buy a condo on the beach.

Unless it's forbidden by the original partnership agreement, you can do that.

Maybe you have another friend who turned down the original deal and now he's sorry, because Joe and his pizzeria are so successful.

So you go that friend and negotiate a deal. You sell him your share of the Limited Partnership for whatever amount of money the two of you agree is fair.

Maybe $10,000, maybe a lot more. That's between the two of you.

After you accept his money and sign the paperwork, you have no more right to that 5% of Joe's Pizzeria's monthly net profits. They go to your friend while you go swimming at the beach in Florida.

And if Joe mixes up that batch of bad pizza dough a month later, that's tough luck for your friend.

But let's say that you don't know anybody who wants to buy your limited partnership share of Joe's Pizzeria.

What can you do?

Aside from beating the bushes, advertising on Craigslist, listing it with a business broker and otherwise looking around for willing buyers — nothing.

Somebody can buy it from you, but you have to find them through informal channels of friendship or business, or through a listing with a business broker. It could take some time.

But let's say you really want to buy that Florida beach condo and you have enough stock in your brokerage account, what could you do?

Simple, sell the stock. Call your broker. Boom. It's done. You get the funds in three days.

Wouldn't it be nice if you could have sold your share in the limited partnership just like shares of stock, by calling your broker and having someone on the New York Stock Exchange buy it from you right away?

That, in Essence, is What a Master Limited Partnership Is

Limited Partnerships in certain businesses can be bought and sold on stock exchanges just as though they were shares of stock.

Pizzerias are not one of those kinds of businesses, and that's just as well.

Next: More on the history and structure of MLPs.

Chapter 5

History of Master Limited Partnerships

The first publicly traded partnership was Apache Oil Company, launched in 1981. Other oil and gas, and also real estate limited partnerships, followed.

In 1987 Congress passed more legislation to define and limit publicly traded partnerships. This created Section 7704 of the Tax Code.

Sec. 7704(b) allows units of some limited partnerships to sell on stock exchanges and through the secondary market just as though they were common shares of corporations. These are, therefore, Publicly Traded Partnerships (PTP).

However, Not All PTPs are MLPs

Under Section 7704(a), a publicly traded partnership is normally taxed as a corporation. This book is not about PTPs which are taxed as corporations.

Under Section 7704(c), a PTP can be taxed as a partnership if 90% of its income can be classified as passive, "qualified income." That is: interest, dividends, real property rents, gains from the sale or other disposition of real property, income and gains derived from natural resources, gains from the sale or disposition of a capital asset, and income and gains from commodities.

Mineral or natural resources activities include exploration, development, production, mining, refining (including fertilizers), marketing and transportation (including pipelines), of oil and gas, minerals, geothermal energy, or timber.

A PTP that receives 90+% qualifying income from energy and commodity related businesses is an Master Limited Partnership, with a lot of tax benefits.

A PTP not receiving 90+% qualifying income must pay taxes as a corporation.

Some PTPs that did not receive qualifying income were grandfathered. Most of these have since gone private, been acquired or have converted to other business entities. Only two of them are still PTPs.

 And MLPs do not have to pay any income taxes so long as they distribute at least 90% of their earnings to unit holders on a quarterly basis. Those are called Quarterly Required Distributions (QRD).

This makes MLPs "pass-through" entities. The cash passes through their hands into yours. This eliminates the double taxation of income issue that is so unfair to shareholders of corporations, allowing you the investor to keep a lot more cash.

By around 1995, however, there were only six MLPs listed on the stock exchanges.

However, the structure has gradually become more popular with energy companies and better-known to investors. Now, around seventy Master Limited Partnerships are available.

In President Bush's 2008 Emergency Economic Stabilization Act (EESA) (P.L. 110-343) — also known as TARP or "the bailout bill" — the definition of qualifying income was expanded. MLPs can now earn income and gains from industrial carbon dioxide; the transportation and storage of alcohol and biodiesel fuel mixtures; some alternative fuels; neat alcohol not derived from alcohol, gas, or coal or having a proof under 190; and neat biodiesel.

Therefore, MLPs can now adapt to "green" power as necessary in the future, and still receive the benefit of no taxation.

Next: why it's good for you to invest in a company that doesn't have to pay taxes.

Avoids future overexposure

Chapter 6

No Taxes on Master Limited Partnerships Means More Money for You

You can probably figure out the general benefit of owning a piece of a business that doesn't have to pay taxes, but I want to go into detail because so many Americans don't understand how unfair the double taxation of corporate income is.

Double Taxation of Corporate Dividends Explained

You own 100 shares of the XYZ Corporation. Let's say that's 1% of the total shares of the corporation. The XYZ Corporation figures out that their 2010 net income is $1 million. Logically and technically, 1% of that — $10,000 — belongs to you.

However, the XYZ Corporation has to pay income taxes on that $1 million. For the purposes of illustrating this point, let's say they have to pay 35%, which is $350,000. They write that check to the IRS and send it in with their tax return.

Therefore, they have $650,000 left.

Remember — your 100 shares of XYZ stock makes you a 1% owner of the corporation. So you as 1% owner just paid $3,500 in taxes to the IRS. You as 1% owner now have $6,500 remaining inside XYZ Inc's bank account.

XYZ Corporation's Board of Directors votes a 50% payout dividend, which is generally as generous a dividend as a corporation is ever going to pay. Soon after, you get a check for $3,250. That's one-half of the remaining $6,500.

If the corporation didn't have to pay income taxes, you'd be getting $5000 (One half of $1 million × 1%).

But now that you've gotten your $3,250 dividend check — guess what?

The IRS wants some of that money too!

In effect, as a 1% owner of the XYZ Corporation, you have already paid $3.500 in taxes.

Yet now that you've gotten a $3,250 check with your name on it, the IRS wants a cut of that too.

So it's true that dividend investors get whacked twice by the IRS.

One of the great things about Master Limited Partnerships is that they don't pay taxes. Of course, you do. But you'll receive a lot more income from them on which to pay the taxes.

But just what do these businesses do to create so much cash flow?

Chapter 7

The Business of Master Limited Partnerships

The business of energy (oil, coal, and natural gas) is technical and complicated.

However, it can be boiled down to three components:

1. The beginning (upstream)

2. The middle (midstream)

3. The end (downstream)

The beginning consists of exploration (finding the energy source) and then extraction (digging or pumping it out of the ground).

The middle consists of processing (refining), storing and transporting the energy from the beginning to the end.

The end of course is when it's sold to the end user. You buy gas at your local gas station. You pay your gas bill to a local utility company.

The beginning and the end get all the attention.

Perhaps that's just a natural result of human perception. If you're given ten items to remember, you'll remember the first ones and the last ones but struggle with the middle ones.

The beginning of the energy business is romantic and dramatic. Texas wildcatters gambling their fortunes on the next big oil field and Arab sheiks riding around on camels.

The end of the energy business gets our attention every time we fill up at the gas station or pay our light and gas bills.

Yet we tend to forget that, between the two, lies a huge infrastructure. We normally take it for granted.

Getting Gas and Oil From There to Here

In the U.S., 280,000 miles of pipelines transport 63 billion cubic feet of natural gas. About 25% are held as Master Limited Partnerships. Another network of 100,000 miles of pipes hauls 20 million barrels of crude oil daily. About 70% of that belongs to MLPs.

Crude oil must also be refined. Gas is processed into Liquified Natural Gas (LNG). It must be transported, often in special tankers. These products must be stored until they're used. And so on.

Some MLPs are also involved with the exploration and production phases of energy.

If you want to invest in "energy" because we're running out of easy supplies of it while world demand is growing, I certainly can't and won't argue with that logic.

However, you'll face ups and downs in energy prices.

If you stick to energy infrastructure MLPs ("midstream"), you'll make money from the entire energy process no matter what the price of a barrel of oil is.

The pipelines are regulated by the Federal Energy Regulatory Commission (FERC).

When they started, FERC set a certain tariff. That is, companies shipping their oil and natural gas through the pipes pay a certain amount per volume.

Every year, that amount goes up based on the Producer Price Index (PPI) for Finished Goods — which is the business version of the Consumer Price Index (CPI) — plus an additional 1.3%. That is set by the 1992 Congressional Energy Policy Act. The rate increase goes into effect on July 1 of every year.

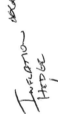

So MLPs make money so long as the production companies wish to transport oil and gas to the end consumer. The price they charge goes up every year more than the rate of inflation.

This is a more favorable form of regulation than utilities face.

Utility Companies Face Stiffer Regulation Than MLPs

If an electric company finds a way to reduce operating costs for a coal-fired electric power plant by 50%, they're required to pass the savings along to the consumers who will be happy to see their electric bills go down.

However, if a pipeline MLP discovered how to lower operating costs, the price per cubic foot it charges remains unchanged. Therefore, lowering operating costs increases its net income.

Their profits go down only when the volume of oil and natural gas that the energy companies need transported goes down.

This can and does, to a degree, happen in economic bad times.

The 2008-2009 Recession was Hard on Master Limited Partnerships

However, they suffered a lot less than the overall stock and bond markets.

13% of MLPs did cut quarterly distributions — for the first time in MLP history. But that also means that 87% maintained or raised their dividends despite the recession.

There were no MLP Initial Public Offerings in 2009. Six MLPs were delisted due to restructuring and bankruptcy. Two of those six were bought out by other MLPs. The other four were taken private or declared bankruptcy.

Because MLPs have to distribute at least 90% of their cash to unit holders, they must continually request new capital from the markets. This forces them to remain competitive.

Although 2008-2009 was a time the credit markets "froze," many MLPs were able to secure financing, though at a higher cost than previously.

Future Energy Infrastructure Needs

But common sense tells you that society needs energy. Even in recessions, people turn on their lights, drive to the store and heat their homes during winter.

Also, most interstate pipelines have contracts with firm commitments. The producers must pay whether they actually transport oil or gas or not.

Some experts believe that overall demand for energy in the United States will continue to go up 1% per year. It's expected that in the U.S. $100 billion of new pipelines will be built.

According to The Interstate Natural Gas Association of America (INGAA), from 2009 to 2030, "a total of $133 to $210 billion must be spent on all types of midstream natural gas infrastructure."

According to Swank Capital, LLC, 80% of this will be for natural gas transmission pipelines, and they expect MLPs to build the majority of these projects.

They've identified important new shale natural gas basins:

Barnett Shale Texas
Woodford Shale Oklahoma
Fayetteville Shale Arkansas
Marcellus Shale Pennsylvania
Rockies Colorado, Wyoming, Utah
Eagle Ford South Texas
Haynesville East Texas / Louisiana

Because of growing production in oil sands of Canada, there's a growing need to ship crude oil from Canada to refineries in the Rockies, the Midwest and the Gulf Coast.

Midstream MLPs collect money from transporting crude oil, refined product and natural gas no matter how much the production company has to pay to extract the energy or how much the end consumer has to pay for it.

MLP physical assets tend to have a long life. Pipelines installed before World War 2 are still operating. There's low risk of technological obsolescence. A piece of pipe is pretty much a piece of pipe. And modern pipes come with rust coatings and cathodic protection that will probably keep them in service for one hundred years or more.

However, because it's expensive to install entire new networks of pipelines and storage facilities, there is a high barrier to entry.

But what good are Master Limited Partnerships to the larger energy corporations that create them in the first place?

Chapter 8

Why Energy Companies Want to Create Master Limited Partnerships

Historically, the energy companies put their focus on the beginning (exploration and production) and the end (selling the product to consumers) of the energy process.

They make their money by finding and working the original sources, the oil wells and mines and by selling the end result to the consumer at the gas station.

The middle levels of refining, transporting and storage are important but were never considered profit points. They were just necessary steps to get the oil or gas from under the ground to the consumer. The energy companies saw their money come in at Points A and Z — not Points B through Y.

The law authorizing MLPs changed that perspective. The pipelines or storage facilities can be transferred to a limited partnership controlled by the energy company, which controls the MLP's General Partner.

They Raise Additional Funds from the Initial Public Offering

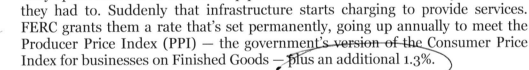

They spent millions of dollars on pipelines and other infrastructure just because they had to. Suddenly that infrastructure starts charging to provide services. FERC grants them a rate that's set permanently, going up annually to meet the Producer Price Index (PPI) — the government's version of the Consumer Price Index for businesses on Finished Goods — plus an additional 1.3%.

Profits are tax-free so long as 90% or more of cash is shared with unit holders.

The GP starts with a 2% share of the MLP but, if it does a good job, can over time raise that up to 50%.

These are called Incentive Distribution Rights. (Some MLPs have this capped at 25%). They align the GP's financial interest with that of the MLP.

What used to be millions of dollars worth of capital equipment needing upgrades and repairs is now a profit center bringing in additional big bucks. Sweet.

When a big company makes some of its assets into an MLP, that's called a roll out.

When multiple, small companies consolidate themselves into an MLP, that's a roll up.

When a company puts new assets into an MLP, that's a roll in.

According to Alerian, there's still about $200 billion worth of energy infrastructure that could be brought to market within an MLP structure.

The MLP Structure

However, most General Partners are not the corporation which created the MLP.

In most cases the corporation creates a limited liability company (LLC). The corporation owns the LLC, but the LLC is the GP of the MLP.

If anything goes wrong with the MLP, the GP is responsible. But if, therefore, the GP is an LLC, its liability is limited. (That's why they call them "limited" liability companies.)

The MLP would suffer financially and so would the LLC, but not the corporation that really controls both of them.

Remember the example of Joe's Pizzeria? If the pizzeria is a limited liability company — even if Joe is the only owner — when the customers with green hair sues, they must sue the LLC itself. Any assets of the LLC (money in the LLC's bank account, the pizza oven) can be seized and given to the customers.

But Joe's personal money and house are safe. Operating the pizzeria as an LLC limits his liability for damages to the assets of the business — it keeps his personal assets safe.

(Therefore, everybody in business by themselves should operate as a limited liability company, to protect their personal assets and property from their business liabilities.)

The General Partner and Limited Partners (LP)

In Master Limited Partnerships there is one General Partner (GP), usually an LLC 100% owned by an energy related corporation and many Limited Partners (LP) who have bought units of the partnership.

The GP starts out with 2% ownership of the MLPs. This means that when quarterly distributions are made, the GP receives 2% of the cash.

However, the GP also has Incentive Distribution Rights (IDR).

This means that if they run the company well and it meets certain levels of success, over time the GP's ownership percentage increases.

This does dilute LP equity in the MLP as a whole. However, the GP does not get any additional ownership unless it's producing a steady stream of cash for the LPs.

However, the GP's allowable share of ownership in the LP is fifty percent. Some MLPs have it capped at twenty-five percent.

Because the GP has total control over and management of how the MLP functions as a business, there could be a conflict of interest. In their book Yes, You Can Be A Successful, Income Investor: Reaching for Yield in Today's Market by Ben Stein and Phil DeMuth express this concern over the MLP structure.

The purpose of the IDRs is to give the GP an incentive to run the company well. If they can get nothing in return except 2% of the distributions, they won't perform as well, goes the thinking behind the law.

Personally, I don't see much of a practical difference — for small investors — between this aspect of MLPs and corporations.

Yes, owners of common stock in a corporation have the right to attend shareholder meetings and vote on rules and the Board of Directors. And if you own enough millions of dollars of stock maybe you can even change something you don't like.

And MLP unit holders don't have those rights.

But those of us who aren't corporate raiders or reformers are stuck with companies we don't and can't control.

Being owners of common stock didn't help the shareholders of Enron.

My opinion is that if a company's officers are going to run the company for their own personal benefit at my expense, they're going to do it whether the company is structured as an MLP or a corporation. There's nothing I can do about it anyway except to diversify.

Some General Partners are Also Publicly Traded MLPs

Where it gets complicated is that some of the MLPs you'll see listed in this book have General Partners which are NOT LLCs — they're publicly traded MLPs in their own right.

That is, you can buy units in those MLPs from your broker just as you can in the first MLP.

Even though their only "business" is managing the first MLP.

Thus, A LP operates a natural gas pipeline business. You can buy units in A LP and share in its profits.

Like all MLPs must, A LP has a General Partner which owns 2% of it (plus incentive distribution rights up to 50% total) and which actually runs the business.

Unlike the first situation I described above, the GP of A LP is also an MLP. It usually has a name such as A GP LP. (You'll spot examples of this when you read the pages on individual Master Limited Partnerships at the end of this book.)

You can buy units in A GP LP from your broker. You'll receive quarterly distributions which are actually taken from its GP ownership of A LP.

As every MLP must, A GP LP has its own General Partner. This is probably an LLC which is 100% owned by the energy corporation that originally owned the assets of A LP.

This allows the corporation to raise more money from investors when offering new MLP units for sale to the marketplace.

However, it also allows unit holders to receive more quarterly distributions from the underlying business of transporting natural gas.

Next: a few energy industry related terms defined.

Chapter 9

A Few Energy-Industry Technical Terms Explained

I don't want to turn this book into some kind of primer on the petroleum industry, but a brief overview of it and some of the technical terms I use when describing Master Limited Partnerships will help you understand them better.

1. Upstream

This refers to activities geared to finding and producing the energy source. You also see references to "Exploration and Production," which are fairly self-explanatory.

Finding oil fields, drilling for oil and pumping oil and natural gas from them are included here.

Some MLPs are involved in this sector, but it's a lot more volatile. You can waste a lot of money drilling for oil that isn't there. Some oil fields run out of oil. And the world market price for oil jumps up and down.

2. Midstream

After oil and gas are taken out of the ground, they must be processed and refined and actually transported to the people and businesses that use them.

A lot of midstream MLPs own "gathering lines" for natural gas. The wells drill down for the gas, and the pressure forces it up into these gathering lines. The gathering lines link the wells with central collection points and processing plants.

A lot of midstream MLPs own and operate these processing plants. They remove natural gas liquids (NGL), water, carbon dioxide and sulfur.

Then they transport the natural gas through high strength steel pipes 20 to 42 inches in diameter.

Every seventy miles or so, a compressor station must boost the pressure to keep the gas flowing.

Some natural gas must go to places that cannot be reached by a pipeline. Therefore, it's made extremely cold, reducing its volume by a factor of 600. This Liquified Natural Gas (LNG) is shipped in special tankers.

Crude oil is refined into types of gasolene, propane and other petroleum products. Then it too is shipped, driven or piped to the end consumers.

Midstream is where most MLPs operate most of the time, and where I suggest you focus your investment dollars.

3. Downstream

The gas, refined oil products and natural gas eventually reaches the end consumer.

This could be utility companies that burn it to generate electricity or send it into our homes to keep our water hot.

It can be gasoline stations where we fill up our gas tanks.

It can be residential or commercial customers of heating oil or propane gas.

Some MLPs operate in this area, especially those that sell heating oil or propane through retail outlets.

Next: The National Association of Publicly Traded Partnerships (NAPTP)

Chapter 10

The National Association of Publicly Traded Partnerships

The National Association of Publicly Traded Partnerships (NAPTP) is a trade organization representing all publicly traded partnerships and publicly traded limited liability companies (LLC) taxed as partnerships.

All Master Limited Partnerships are represented by this trade organization (formerly the Coalition of Publicly Traded Partnerships). However, not all publicly traded partnerships are Master Limited Partnerships. That term is reserved for those with qualifying income from natural resources and energy so they are tax-free as long as they pay out 90% or more cash distributions to their unit holders.

Not all publicly traded partnerships meet this definition. Some are in other industry sectors. For example, some equity management organizations such as the Blackstone Group (NYSE: BX) and Fortress Investment Group (NYSE: FIG) are structured as publicly traded partnerships. Of the 90 PTPs, about 70 are Master Limited Partnerships.

NAPTP works to protect the current tax status of PTPs, enacting legislation to improve their legal status, and prevent states from enacting tax provisions that are difficult or impossible for PTPs to comply with. As an investor in MLPs, you don't need or want to care much about NAPTP and its activities. However, its website is a good resource for information on MLPs. And it's good to know that someone is looking for legal ways to protect and benefit MLPs.

And they do have a lot of information useful to MLP investors, such as state tax information.

Website

naptp.org/

Now that we know they have a professional trade group looking after their interests, how do we evaluate MLPs on the whole?

Chapter 11

Master Limited Partnership Indexes

The usual way for investors to evaluate investments is to look at an index.

The Dow Jones Industrial Average is an index consisting of 30 of the most prominent companies in the stock market.

The S&P 500 is the five hundred largest companies, so it's more representative of the broad stock market than is the DJIA.

There're many indexes of all kinds of different stocks, bonds and other financial securities.

Master Limited Partnerships have five:

1. **Alerian MLP Index**

2. **Citigroup® MLP Index**

3. **Cushing® 30 MLP Index**

4. **Standard & Poor's MLP Index**

5. **Tortoise MLP Index**

6. **Wells Fargo Securities, LLC MLP Index**

Chapter 11-A

Alerian MLP Index (AMZ)

Alerian Capital Management LLC is a registered investment adviser that manages portfolios for both institutional and individual clients. They focus on midstream MLPs. I believe that their index is the most closely watched in this industry.

It is derived from the fifty most prominent MLPs in the energy sector and calculated by Standard & Poor's using a float-adjusted market capitalization methodology.

A company must be a Master Limited Partnership in production, transportation, processing, or storage of energy commodities. It must trade on the New York Stock Exchange, EuroNext (formerly the American Stock Exchange) Exchange or NASDAQ exchange. It must have at least four quarters of distributions equal to or greater than its Minimum Quarterly Distribution (MQD). It must be above $5 per unit in price. It must have a market cap over $500 million.

The base date for AMZ is December 29, 1995 with a base value of 100.

AMZ is the ticker symbol for the price index.

AMZX is the ticker symbol for the total return index.

This index does not include General Partner shares or tradable, non-common units.

The AMZ Index Companies

Alliance Holdings GP LP
AmeriGas Partners LP
Alliance Resource Partners LP
Buckeye GP Holdings LP
Buckeye Partners LP
Boardwalk Pipeline Partners LP
Calumet Specialty Products Partners LP
Copano Energy LLC
Duncan Energy Partners LP
Dorchester Minerals LP
DCP Midstream Partners LP

Enbridge Energy Partners LP
Enbridge Energy Management LLC
Encore Energy Partners LP
El Paso Pipeline Partners LP
Enterprise Products Partners LP
Enterprise GP Holdings LP
Energy Transfer Equity LP
Energy Transfer Partners LP
EV Energy Partners LP
Ferrellgas Partners LP
Genesis Energy LP
Holly Energy Partners LP
Kinder Morgan Energy Partners LP
Kinder Morgan Management LLC
Legacy Reserves LP
Linn Energy LLC
Magellan Midstream Partners LP
MarkWest Energy Partners LP
Targa Resources Partners LP
Navios Maritime Partners LP
Inergy LP
Natural Resource Partners LP
NuStar Energy LP
NuStar GP Holdings LLC
ONEOK Partners LP
Plains All American Pipeline LP
Pioneer Southwest Energy Partners LP
Penn Virginia GP Holdings LP
Penn Virginia Resource Partners LP
Regency Energy Partners LP
Spectra Energy Partners LP
Suburban Propane Partners LP
Sunoco Logistics Partners LP
TC Pipelines LP
Teekay LNG Partners LP
Teekay Offshore Partners LP
Western Gas Partners LP
Williams Pipeline Partners LP
Williams Partners LP

An important subset of AMZ is the Alerian MLP Infrastructure Index which includes only MLPs with midstream energy transportation and storage assets. The ticker symbol is AMZI.

The AMZI index

Buckeye Partners LP
Boardwalk Pipeline Partners LP
Calumet Specialty Products Partners LP
Copano Energy LLC
Duncan Energy Partners LP
DCP Midstream Partners LP
Enbridge Energy Partners LP
El Paso Pipeline Partners LP
Enterprise Products Partners LP
Energy Transfer Partners LP
Genesis Energy LP
Kinder Morgan Energy Partners LP
Magellan Midstream Partners LP
MarkWest Energy Partners LP
Targa Resources Partners LP
NuStar Energy LP
ONEOK Partners LP
Plains All American Pipeline LP
Regency Energy Partners LP
Spectra Energy Partners LP
Sunoco Logistics Partners LP
TC Pipelines LP
Western Gas Partners LP
Williams Pipeline Partners LP
Williams Partners LP

Website

alerian.com/insight.html

Chapter 11-B

Citigroup® MLP Index (CITIMLP)

CITIMLP began in July 2006 and consists of leading natural resource-related master limited partnerships.

CITIMLP is the ticker symbol for the price index.

CITIMLPT is the ticker symbol for the total return index.

Companies in this index must be exchange-traded Master Limited Partnerships in the natural resource sector and have a market capitalization of at least $500 million.

The index goes back to December 31, 1999 with a base value of 100. It is handled by Dow Jones and weighted by market capitalization.

Chapter 11-C

Cushing® 30 MLP Index (MLPX)

Swank Energy Income Advisers created this index to track midstream MLP performance.

The Cushing 30 is an equal weighted index comprised of 30 publicly listed, midstream Master Limited Partnerships. It's calculated by Standard & Poor's based on an objective, formula-based propriety system set out by Swank Energy Income Advisers.

Companies must be MLPs in the energy natural resources sector of transportation, storage, gathering and processing; be publicly traded; meet certain financial criteria that emphasizes earnings and distributions; and be paying a current distribution.

It deliberately excludes energy companies that are sensitive to fluctuations in the market price of commodities and the more volatile shipping and upstream MLPs.

The Cushing 30 MLP Index

Alliance Resource Partners
AmeriGas Partners LP
Boardwalk Pipeline Partners
Buckeye Partners LP
Copano Energy LLC
Duncan Energy Partners LP
El Paso Pipeline Partners LP
Enbridge Energy Partners LP
Energy Transfer Equity LP
Energy Transfer Partners LP
Enterprise GP Holdings LP
Enterprise Product Partners LP
Genesis Energy LP
Inergy LP
Kinder Morgan Energy Part LP
Magellan Midstream Partners
Markwest Energy Partners LP
Natural Resource Partners LP
NuStar Energy LP

Master Limited Partnerships

NuStar GP Holdings LLC
ONEOK Partners LP
Plains All American Pipeline LP
Regency Energy Partners LP
SPECTRA ENERGY PARTNERS LP
Sunoco Logistics Partners LP
TARGA RESOURCES PARTNERS LP
TC Pipelines LP
Western Gas Partners LP
Williams Partners LP
Williams Pipeline Partners L

Website

cushingmlpindex.com/

Chapter 11-D

Standard & Poor's MLP Index (SPMLP)

The S&P MLP Index is designed to track the value of Master Limited Partnerships and publicly traded limited liability companies. It focuses on companies operating under the Global Industry Classification Standard (GICS) Energy Sector (Code 10) and the GICS Gas Utilities Industry (Code 551020).

The index uses modified market capitalization-weighting to reflect available float, reduce single stock concentration and enhance liquidity of the overall index. No one stock can comprise more than 15% of the index.

The company must have a market cap above $300 million. And daily volume for the past three months must average over $2 million. They must be listed on the New York Stock Exchange or NASDAQ Exchange.

The index is rebalanced once a year, after the third Friday in July. The base value of the index is 1000 starting July 20, 2001.

The ticker symbol for the market value of the index is SPMLP. The ticker symbol for the total return value of the index is SPMLPT.

Top 10 Companies in SPMLP

Kinder Morgan Energy Partners LP
Enterprise Product Partners LP
Energy Transfer Partners LP
Energy Transfer Equity LP
Plains All American Pipeline LP
Enbridge Energy Partners LP
ONEOK Partners LP
Kinder Morgan Management LLC
Boardwalk Pipeline Partners
Linn Energy LLC

Website

standardandpoors.com/indices/sp-mlp/en/us/?indexId=sp-master-limited-partnership-index

Chapter 11-E

Tortoise MLP Index™ (TMLP)

Tortoise Capital Advisers LLC maintains the Tortoise MLP Index. Its ticker symbol for the price index is TMLP. Its ticker symbol for the total return index is TMLPT. TMLP starts with December 31, 1999 and a base value of 100. Standard & Poor's calculates the index. It's rebalanced quarterly.

It is a float-adjusted, capitalization weighted index of publicly traded MLPs engaged in the transportation, production, processing, and/or storage of energy commodities. Basically, almost every MLP this book is concerned with is included in the Tortoise index. There's apparently no restrictions except that the MLP be publicly traded and in the energy infrastructure sector. No one company can constitute more than 10% of the total index.

TMLP companies currently are:

Alliance Holdings GP LP
Alliance Resource Partners LP
Amerigas Partners LP
Atlas Pipeline Partners LP
Boardwalk Pipeline Partners LP
BreitBurn Energy Partners LP
Buckeye GP Holdings LP
Buckeye Partners LP
Calumet Specialty Products Partners LP
Capital Product Partners LP
Cheniere Energy Partners LP
Copano Energy LLC
DCP Midstream Partners LP
Dorchester Minerals LP
Duncan Energy Partners LP
EV Energy Partner LP
Eagle Rock Energy Partners LP
El Paso Pipeline Partners LP
Enbridge Energy Management LLC
Enbridge Energy Partners LP
Encore Energy Partners LP
Energy Transfer Equity LP
Energy Transfer Partners LP

Enterprise GP Holdings LP
Enterprise Products Partners LP
Exterran Partners LP
Ferrellgas Partners LP
Genesis Energy LP
Global Partners LP/MA
Holly Energy Partners LP
Inergy Holdings LP
Inergy LP
K-Sea Transportation Partners LP
Kinder Morgan Energy Partners LP
Kinder Morgan Management LLC
Legacy Reserves LP
Linn Energy LLC
Magellan Midstream Partners LP
MarkWest Energy Partners LP
Martin Midstream Partners LP
Natural Resource Partners LP
NuStar Energy LP
NuStar GP Holdings LLC
ONEOK Partners LP
Pioneer Southwest Energy Partners LP
Penn Virginia GP Holdings LP
Penn Virginia Resource Partners LP
Plains All American Pipeline LP
Quicksilver Gas Services LP
Regency Energy Partners LP
Spectra Energy Partners LP
Star Gas Partners LP
Suburban Propane Partners LP
Sunoco Logistics Partners LP
Targa Resources Partners LP
TC Pipelines LP
Teekay LNG Partners LP
Teekay Offshore Partners LP
Transmontaigne Partners LP
Vanguard Natural Resources LLC
Western Gas Partners LP
Williams Partners LP
Williams Pipeline Partners LP

Website

tortoiseadvisors.com/tortoise-mlp-index.cfm

Chapter 11-F

Wells Fargo (formerly Wachovia) Midstream MLP Index

It's a float-adjusted, capitalization-weighted index of energy Master Limited Partnerships or limited liability companies acting as the general partner of an MLP with a market capitalization of at least $200 million at the time it's added to the index and a trading history of at least 60 days. If an MLP goes below that market cap of $200 million it's removed from the index (which is reviewed quarterly).

They must also be listed on the New York Stock Exchange, the NYSE EuroNext Exchange (formerly the American Stock Exchange) or the NASDAQ Exchange.

Wachovia Capital Markets, LLC began publishing the Wachovia MLP Composite Index December 11, 2006. At that time it consisted of 43 energy MLPs including 6 general partnerships (GP).

The ticker symbol for the market prices is WMLP.

The total return index's ticker symbol is WMLPT.

Wells Fargo took control of this index in the disastrous days of the 2008 financial crisis when it bought out Wachovia.

Wachovia went back to December 29, 1989, the very early days of MLPs, and used that with a base value of 100. (This was independently calculated in 1999 by Standard & Poor's.) It's divided into ten sectors.

The 10 Sectors

Coal
Oil Pipeline
Gathering, Processing, and NGLs
Marine Transportation
Natural Gas Pipeline
Oil and Gas
Oilfield Services
Propane

Refined Products
Refining

You can see that, despite the name of the index, some of these sectors include energy production (the "Oil and Gas "sector) and retail sales ("Propane").

The index is valued on a price-return basis as well as a total-return basis. Therefore it reflects the value of owning MLPs and receiving their distributions as well as simple rises in the market price of their units.

As of this writing, the Wells Fargo Index consists of:

1. Alliance Holdings GP LP
2. Alliance Resource Partners
3. AmeriGas Partners LP
4. Atlas Pipeline Partners LP
5. Boardwalk Pipeline Partners, LP
6. BreitBurn Energy Partners LP
7. Buckeye GP Holdings LP
8. Buckeye Partners LP
9. Calumet Specialty Products Partners LP
10. Capital Product Partners LP
11. Cheniere Energy Partners LP
12. Copano Energy LLC
13. Crosstex Energy LP
14. DCP Midstream Partners LP
15. Dorchester Minerals LP
16. Duncan Energy Partners LP
17. EV Energy Partner LP
18. Eagle Rock Energy Partners LP
19. El Paso Pipeline Partners LP
20. Enbridge Energy Management LLC
21. Enbridge Energy Partners LP
22. Encore Energy Partners-LP
23. Energy Transfer Equity LP
24. Energy Transfer Partners LP
25. Enterprise GP Holdings LP
26. Enterprise Product Partners LP
27. Exterran Partners LP
28. Ferrellgas Partners LP
29. Genesis Energy LP
30. Global Partners LP
31. Holly Energy Partners LP
32. Inergy Holdings LP
33. Inergy LP

34. K-Sea Transportation Partners LP
35. Kinder Morgan Energy Part LP
36. Kinder Morgan Management LLC
37. LEGACY RESERVES LP
38. Linn Energy LLC
39. Magellan Midstream Partners, L.P.
40. Markwest Energy Partners LP
41. Martin Midstream Partners LP
42. Natural Resource Partners LP
43. Navios Maritime Partners LP
44. NuStar Energy LP
45. NuStar GP Holdings LLC
46. ONEOK Partners LP
47. Pioneer Southwest Energy Partners L.P.
48. Penn Virginia GP Holdings LP
49. Penn Virginia Resource Partners LP
50. Plains All American Pipeline LP
60. Quicksilver Gas Services LP
61. Regency Energy Partners LP
62. SPECTRA ENERGY PARTNERS LP
63. Star Gas Partners LP
64. Suburban Propane Partners LP
65. Sunoco Logistics Partners LP
66. TARGA RESOURCES PARTNERS LP
67. TC Pipelines LP
68. Teekay LNG Partners LP
69. Teekay Offshore Partners LP
70. Transmontaigne Partners LP
71. Vanguard Natural Resources, LLC
72. Western Gas Partners LP
73. Williams Partners LP
74. Williams Pipeline Partners LP

Website

wachoviaresearch.com/C7/Indices/default.aspx

Now let's return to the best part of Master Limited Partnerships — the money it sends to us MLP investors.

Chapter 12

Distributable Cash Flow

How do Master Limited Partnerships figure out how much cash to send you every quarter?

That is called "distributable cash flow" (DCF).

First, they figure out their net income as any business would.

Sales (income) minus expenses equals net income.

However, remember that "expenses" includes a substantial amount of non-cash depreciation and amortization (which is similar to depreciation) expenses on their equipment. They use Generally Accepted Accounting Principles (GAAP) and government regulations.

To figure out how much actual cash it has left, the MLP adds those depreciation and amortization figures back into net income.

They also have to estimate how much they'll have to pay — in cash, out of pocket — for actual maintenance and repair expenses. When you own a lot of pipelines, refineries and other complicated oil and natural gas equipment, it's a large amount.

However, for most MLPs the depreciation expense is much larger.

Therefore, the end result for DCF is generally much higher than most corporations could afford to pay. That's true even of utilities, banks, consumer brand names and real estate investment trusts — the traditional "high yield" types of dividend stocks.

Right now, MLPs beat them all.

But by now, you may be wondering how and why MLPs continue to have such high yields.

Chapter 13

Why MLP Market Prices Aren't Higher, Reducing Yields

Some investors may well question why, if Master Limited Partnerships are such a great investment, their yields continue to remain so high compared to other high yield investments such as real estate investment trusts (REIT).

If MLPs are such a good thing, why aren't more people buying them and driving up their prices?

One answer lies in the lack of institutional support for MLPs. Right now, about 90% of MLP units are owned by individuals, not institutions.

MLPs Present Mutual Funds With Practical Problems

For mutual funds, distributions from MLPs were considered non-qualifying sources of income, which impedes regulated investment companies (RIC) from buying them.

Therefore, mutual funds could not buy MLPs until a codicil (Section 331) to the 2004 American Jobs Creation Act allowed them to invest up to 25% of their assets in non-qualifying sources of income so long as they don't own any more than 10% of any one particular company.

However, they have not done so because of practical matters.

Partly it's simple paperwork. Mutual funds are required to send out 1099s in January. Yet, because K-1 partnership forms aren't sent out until February or even March, the mutual funds couldn't put accurate information on the 1099s. They could guess, but they'd have to send out amended 1099s, angering customers who'd already filed their tax returns.

Plus, there's the issue of IRAs. If you're a mutual fund manager you want people to open IRA accounts with your mutual fund. They can't do that if your mutual fund shares will generate more than $1,000 in Unrelated Business Taxable Income (UBTI) (I.R.C. §§511-514).

Hedge funds have bought into MLPs, and that reached a peak in 2007. In 2008 and 2009 they had to sell their units to deleverage during the financial crisis.

MLPs do not fit well into the exchange traded fund (ETF) format, because every owner of ETF shares would have to be sent a K-1 form for every MLP owned by the fund. This would greatly discourage ownership of that ETF. That is why Bear Stearns, before they nearly went out of business, and now JPMorgan have issued Exchange Traded Notes (ETN) for MLPs. However, they are not the same thing.

Funds Do Not Pay Taxes, so They're Not Concerned With the Tax Advantages of MLPs

A lot of stock market money comes from institutions: mutual funds, pension funds, life insurance funds and trust funds. Because they're tax-exempt, they don't have the same motivation to buy up Master Limited Partnerships.

Therefore, when you buy MLP units you're not competing with the Big Money, only other individuals.

Many of those individual invest only with their tax-exempt retirement funds, and so they don't buy MLPs.

Plus, there's been a shortage of generally available information on the opportunity presented by MLPs.

And plus, many investors who are aware of MLPs and do have taxable brokerage accounts just don't want the extra work at tax time.

This means there's a lot of opportunity for you to buy MLPs with high yields.

But you'll have to understand the tax complications.

Chapter 14

Huge Obstacle? Or Huge Opportunity?

Do you see the glass as half full or half empty?

If you know much about military strategy, martial arts, sports or chess, you're familiar with the concept that any strength can be a weakness and used against you.

This type of strength-as-weakness situation describes Master Limited Partnerships and taxes.

One of the benefits of MLPs that I find exciting is also what a lot of ordinary investors dislike about MLPs, despite their many benefits — taxes.

MLPs Own a Lot of Physical Assets, Such as Pipelines and Other Energy-Related Types of Infrastructure

Physical assets, like everything in this entropy-dominated universe, don't last forever. Their useful life is limited.

Now, nobody truly knows what the useful life of any particular piece of pipe or valve is, any more than anybody truly knows the future of any particular financial security or market.

Some of the pipeline currently in use was installed before World War 2. Pipes installed today use special rust coatings and cathodic protection. they're virtually indestructible and so may last one hundred years or more.

The government recognizes that physical assets go downhill and must eventually be replaced. Therefore, Generally Accepted Accounting Principles and IRS regulations specify that every year a company may count a certain percentage of the cost of its physical assets as an expense.

This is called depreciation.

Depreciation Example

A quick example will make the idea clearer. Say a company buys a widget machine today for $50,000, and they expect (and Generally Accepted Accounting Principles and the government allow) its useful life will be 10 years. In ten years they'll need to buy a new widget machine.

So in this year and the next nine, the company is allowed to call $5000 a depreciation expense of doing business using that widget machine.

$50,000 divided by 10 equals $5,000 per year.

That is true even though the company has not actually spent any cash out of its pocket and the widget machine is operating just fine.

Maybe once a month they have to pay a mechanic $40 per hour to change the widget machine's oil and replace its rotor blade. That's cash out of the company's pocket for required maintenance. That's another expense, but it has nothing to do with depreciation.

Depreciation assumes that the company will have to replace the widget machine in ten years no matter how well it's maintained.

Because they own lots of physical assets, MLPs take a lot of depreciation expense.

This greatly reduces their net income.

(Remember that net income is what's left over after you subtract all expenses from gross income. The more expenses a company has, the less net income or profit.)

However, remember that depreciation is not a cash expense. It's a bookkeeping entry.

Therefore, that cash is still sitting in their bank account.

And they're required to distribute at least 90% to unit holders every quarter.

On average, 80% of a MLP's cash distributions to unit holders consists of cash that is a net profit only because of depreciation.

The government accounting rules say that money is a "return of capital."

That may sound strange, but just remember that the word "capital" has various meanings. We often use it to mean cash for business, but it also applies to a business' physical equipment bought by such cash.

The $50,000 widget machine is another form of capital.

Return of Capital is Not Income

What the government sees as happening is that the cash freed up from the MLP taking the depreciation expense is still capital. As someone who spent money to buy units — to become a co-owner of the business — you spent your capital (dollars from your bank account).

And now the MLP is sending some of it back to you. Which makes it "return" of capital.

It's productive dollars going back into your pocket.

Therefore, return of capital is NOT taxable income.

But You Can Only Receive a "Return" of Money You Spent

Your capital investment in the MLP is whatever your net payment (minus any brokerage commissions of course) was for your units.

Therefore, all the "return of capital" distributions you receive from the MLP reduces the cost basis of your units. You spent some money to own those units, and 80% of every distribution is a kind of refund of the price you paid.

However, logically, this cannot go below zero.

Return of Capital Example

You buy 100 shares of the EEE MLP for $10 per share — $1,000 total (let's ignore broker commissions).

Your cost basis is $1,000.

Every quarter EEE sends you a check for $62.50. At the end of each year, they tell you 80% of that money — $50 per quarter, $200 for the entire year — is "return of capital."

Therefore, you do NOT pay taxes on $62.50 per quarter, only on the $12.50 that is investment income. That $12.50 is taxed as ordinary income.

Every year, your cost basis is reduced by $200. In five years, it's zero.

You continue to hold on to the units, each quarter receiving $62.50 that is now "free" money. The entire cost you paid for it has been refunded back to you.

From that time on, all the quarterly distributions you receive are income taxable at ordinary rates.

Notice that the MLP refunds your entire investment within five years (not guaranteed but a fair historical average), pays you some additional revenue besides and, from that point on continues to send you more money — indefinitely.

This tremendous tax benefit does come at a price, however. And that's where some people get hung up.

Consequences of the Tax Benefits of MLPs

1. Partnership income and losses is reported to partners for tax purposes in February or March of every year.

Because you're a limited partner of the MLP, you receive a K-1 form from the MLP, not an ordinary 1099-DIV.

I don't know why they're allowed to go out later than 1099-DIVs and W-2s, which are supposed to be received by the end of January, but they are. Take that complaint to the IRS.

The K-1 form is more complicated than 1099s. I have a chapter on tax forms later in this book.

And you have to complete a Schedule E, but for MLPs you can ignore 95% of it. I also cover that form later in this book.

2. You're supposed to report your income from them in every single state that they do business in.

That's why I started this chapter off writing about "huge opportunity or huge burden?"

The MLPs will guide you through this. Almost all of them use a service called Tax Package Support. You can go to their websites to download your K-1 information. It will also fill out all the appropriate forms via Turbo Tax.

Plus, they send you a package of instructions to walk you through the steps.

Plus, they all have customer service representatives you can call and ask for help.

The National Association of Publicly Traded Partnership website contains additional information.

The states in which each MLP operates:

naptp.org/documentlinks/StatesforPTPs.doc

And, unless you own a very large number of units, your taxable income per state will be relatively small — often under the amount of income on which a tax return must be filed. And of course, some states, such as Florida and Nevada, don't have state income taxes.

Table of state income taxes —

taxadmin.org/fta/rate/ind_inc.html

And, because they take so many allowances for depreciation, with many midstream MLPs you officially have a net loss, not a net gain. (Even though you've been cashing generous quarterly dividend checks.) If you have no official income from an MLP, you have no income to report to the states in which it does business.

Filing out a lot of state tax returns is extra hassle. Frankly, I doubt that many people actually do it. Unless a lot of money is involved, I doubt that the states are going to come after you. Many of them may not even understand or track MLP income.

Even the American Institute of Certified Public Accountants, in an article on MLPs, advises accountants to consider the "appropriateness" of state "compliance." In other words, cover your behind by advising the client of this feature, then let them decide to take what's probably a very small risk by ignoring state "compliance."

The Extra Work is a Small Price to Pay for Receiving Such Generous Quarterly Distributions

It's part of receiving the tremendous tax benefits of owning MLPs.

Look at it in perspective. Four times a year the MLP sends you a fat check that's four times as large as you'd receive from any S&P dividend paying corporation and twice as large as you'd receive from any real estate investment trust (REIT).

And, unlike with dividends from corporate stocks and REITs, 80% of that quarterly distribution is tax-free!

So you KEEP a lot more of that cash.

In return, once a year, you go through some extra paperwork.

Look, get a grip.

You work hard forty or more hours a week at your job or business to make the money you invest with, not to mention to pay for your groceries.

MLPs will pay you a LOT more money than any other investment. They're more work at tax time, and that's no fun, but it's not the end of the world either. The work is not as hard or stressful as your job or business.

It's a few extra hours (maybe) spent doing your taxes, but every quarter you get paid a lot of money for those few extra hours of annual paperwork.

And if you're reinvesting dividends as you should be if you're not yet retired, that extra return on your investment will multiply itself over and over again for the rest of your life and for your children and other heirs.

Again, you already know how to work — just work a few extra hours. You sweat a lot more every time you mow your lawn in the summer, but you accept that as part of the price of home ownership.

It won't affect your next evaluation. Your boss isn't looking over your shoulder. You can watch TV or listen to the radio. If you're too tired tonight, do it tomorrow night. The only deadline is April 15.

If You are Retired Already, How Well can You Live on Ordinary Dividends from Stocks and REITs?

The extra return from MLPs can transform your retirement from one of constant worry to one of comfortable security.

Isn't that worth a few hours of extra effort at tax time?

Of course, if you're already so wealthy that you can afford to do everything you want without worrying about the amount of your income — great. Put all your money into municipal bonds and don't file any tax returns at all!

So, unless you've reached that lofty height of financial independence, just tell yourself that you want the extra money from MLPs . . .

MLPs pay extra money because they distribute so much tax-free income.

You have more paperwork at tax time, but that's a small price to pay to receive big distribution checks every quarter.

And, besides, you can always pay an accountant or use Turbo Tax.

The next tax issue related to MLPs is one I have some sympathy for — tax-deferred accounts.

Chapter 15

MLPs in Tax-Deferred Accounts

So what causes this?

People learn about an investment that pays huge quarterly distributions which are 80% tax-free . . .

And the first thing they want to do is figure out how to buy it for their tax-deferred retirement accounts!

That's part of the huge opportunity-huge burden situation.

MLPs are great because they're so tax-favorable.

Wanting to own MLPs inside tax-deferred accounts is like walking down the street in a rain storm with your umbrella keeping you dry, then wanting to buy a second umbrella because it's on sale!

So let me say this straight out —

The optimal, best way to invest in MLPs is to buy and keep the units in a regular, taxable brokerage account.

Once you do anything else, you're watering down their benefits.

If you do buy MLPs inside an IRA or other tax-deferred account, you are not only NOT taking full advantage of their benefits, you're creating a potential problem with the IRA.

When placed inside tax-deferred accounts, income from limited partnerships is considered by the IRS to be Unrelated Business Taxable Income (UBTI) — tax code (I.R.C. §§511-514). If it's a small amount, under $1,000, it doesn't affect your IRA or Roth IRA.

However, over $1,000, it is countable income and taxes must be paid.

The IRA custodian must file IRS form 990T and pay the required taxes from your account. If the UBTI is above $500, the custodian is supposed to file an estimated return. It's likely they would charge you a stiff fee for this service.

Now, understand that it's not illegal to hold MLPs in a tax-deferred account. It's just that if your MLP holdings generate over $1,000 in income counted as UBTI, your custodian is supposed to recognize that and pay the tax and file the form, and the taxes and fee for service to the IRA custodian would come out of your IRA, reducing your portfolio.

There're big questions.

Would your tax-deferred account custodian recognize the situation?

How many MLP units would you have to own to generate over $1,000 in UBTI?

If the MLP units did generate over $1,000 UBTI and your custodian failed to send in the tax, what are the odds the IRS would ever discover that?

In the estimation of the experts in this document —

mhinvest.com/supportArticles/MLP-IRA.pdf

it would take around $5 million of MLP units to generate UBTI over $1,000.

Most of us have IRAs quite a bit smaller than that.

However, I also have to acknowledge that for the cash flow of distributions that arrive after you've recovered the entire initial cost of your investment, a tax-deferred account is desirable.

Therefore, there is a long term advantage to receiving MLP income inside a tax-deferred account.

Also, You Cannot Net Out MLP Losses and Income

Here's another irritating thing about MLPs and taxes. Because they write off so much depreciation and other technical bookkeeping items, it's possible for them to report a (passive) loss to you — even though you've received generous quarterly dividends all year round.

Now, by itself, that's good. It means you don't have to pay any taxes on ANY portion of those quarterly distribution checks.

Where it gets irritating is when you own more than one MLP, and some report (passive) losses and some report (non-passive) income.

It'd be simple, logical and (I believe, but I'm not a lawmaker) fair to add the losses and income together and pay taxes on the net result. If it's a loss, take it from your other income. If it's a positive number, you add it to your other taxable income.

However, under the passive activity rules for PTPs under Sec. 469(k), the passive activity loss limitation rules are applied to MLPs on an entity-by-entity basis.

That is, you cannot reduce your income from MLP #1 by your loss from MLP #2.

You must pay taxes on your income from MLP #1.

All you can do with your loss from MLP #2 is carry it forward. That means, keep track of it. If next year or some other point in the future, MLP #2 reports income, you can apply the past losses to that income, reducing your future tax expense.

Another Possible Tax Wrinkle

The rules under Sec. 469(e)(1) make the situation even more complicated. If MLP #2 has a K-1 Line 1 business loss but income from non-business related income (Lines 5 through 7; Interest through Royalties), you the limited partner still have to pay taxes on THAT income — because it's not related to the MLP's actual business.

The good news is, there are also ways around these issues.

They're not perfect, but they exist.

But first, how to fill out the MLP-related tax forms.

Chapter 16

What You Need to Know If You Do Your Own Taxes — MLP Tax Forms

This chapter comes in four parts.

1. The K-1 form the MLP is required to send you early every year.

2. The IRS Partner's Instructions for Schedule K-1 (Form 1065)

3. Keeping track of losses and your cost basis

4. The Schedule E form you're required to complete when you do your tax return.

(By the way, if you consult those thick income tax instruction books that big accounting companies publish early every year to help you prepare your taxes, you'll find that their info on completing these forms is inadequate, to say the least. For the IRS Form 8582 all two of them say is, "See the (IRS) instructions." Thanks for nothing, guys.)

The Schedule K-1 (Form 8865) Partner's Share of Income, Deductions, Credits, etc. 2009 revision

MLPs are Publicly Traded Partnerships. That is all this chapter will cover. If you are a limited partner in a private limited partnership or receive K-1s for any other reason, see your accountant.

Here is what the latest K-1 form looks like.

www.irs.gov/pub/irs-pdf/f8865sk1.pdf

The K-1 starts out with basic information in Part I. It'll be for the tax year. The MLP must list its employer identification number. Then its name and business address.

Part II will have information about you. Whatever partner identifying number they assigned to you, your name and address.

Section E. Your share of profit, loss, capital and deductions. This will be a certain percentage that depends on how many units of the MLP have been created and how many you own.

Section F. Partner's capital account analysis.

As a partner in the MLP, you have a separate capital account.

The beginning capital amount is the net amount you started off the period with — whatever you paid for your units. In the "Withdrawals and Distributions" block will be the total amount of distributions you received which are considered a "return of capital" and therefore nontaxable.

The "Ending Capital Account" is the end balance remaining.

Once that end balance goes to zero (it could take from four to six years), all distributions you receive from the MLP are taxable as ordinary income.

At that time, the MLP distributions you receive will be simpler to account for, but you'll have to pay more taxes.

Part III is reporting your income to you. It could be positive or a loss.

Line 1 is ordinary business income (or loss).

If any positive amount is shown here, you must put that on Schedule E, line 28, column (j).

For publicly traded partnerships, this income or loss is considered non-passive.

NOTE: Because the MLP will be taking deductions for depreciation and other technical write-offs that do not actually take cash out of their bank account, it's possible for them to have lots of cash to distribute to you and still declare a "loss."

If you have a loss, remember that's good in the sense that you won't pay any taxes on all that money you received from the MLP.

You must keep a record of it, however.

For one thing, if that same MLP has net income next year, you can use this year's loss to reduce next year's net income, saving you money next year.

Partner's Instructions for Schedule K-1 (Form 1065)

These are the IRS instructions to you. I'll just point out the highlights that apply to MLPs. As with many partnership issues, much just does not concern or apply to us.

Here is the IRS version:

www.irs.gov/pub/irs-pdf/i1065sk1.pdf

1. Keep the K-1 form. Don't file it with your tax return. The IRS already has a copy.

2. You are responsible to maintain your own record of your cost basis in the limited partnership. It's no big deal. Just fill out the required worksheet and never throw it away.

3. Do complete the Worksheet for Adjusting the Basis of a Partner's Interest in the Partnership.

On Line 1, put your adjusted basis as figured last year. If you just bought the units, enter 0 (zero) on line 1 and the net amount you paid on Line 2.

Or, if you bought new units, put the new amount on Line 2.

Ignore Lines 3 through 6.

On Line 7, enter the total "Withdrawals and Distributions" figure entered in Section F of the K-1 form.

Ignore Lines 8 through 11.

Add Lines 1 and 2.

Subtract Line 7.

Enter the balance on Line 12. If it's negative, just put zero.

This is your record of the cost basis of your units. It starts out being whatever the net amount you paid for them on the open market.

You receive quarterly cash distributions and, on average, 80% of those are considered "return of capital." (But for any given MLP, can be less or more.)

That return of capital is subtracted from what you paid for the shares.

What's left is your cost basis. It cannot go below zero.

You can then ignore the form until you reach the subheading "Publicly Traded Partnerships," which is another term for MLP.

If the MLP reports a loss for the year, that's considered a passive loss to you.

However, if you have a net gain, that's non-passive income.

Keep Track of Any Losses

Although there's a bewildering number of references to various forms, especially the 8582, Page 12 of the 8582 Passive Loss Limitations Instructions clearly says: "Do not report passive income, gains or losses from a PTP on Form 8585."

They say to use the following instructions. Their examples are immensely confusing because they seem to imply you should use Form 4797, but that's only for selling your units.

Next year when you do your taxes, refer to this year's records. If you have a gain next year, it can be reduced by this year's loss.

If this MLP continues to have losses every year, just let them accumulate. Maybe in ten years you'll have a gain you don't want to be taxed on.

If your MLP never has a gain, the losses just accumulate.

Don't worry, be happy — keep cashing your quarterly distribution checks.

Schedule E Supplemental Income and Loss (From rental real estate, royalties, partnerships, S corporations, estates, trusts, REMICs, etc.)

Here is a sample of 2009 Schedule E:

www.irs.gov/pub/irs-pdf/f1040se.pdf

Here are the 2009 Schedule E instructions:

www.irs.gov/pub/irs-pdf/i1040se.pdf

(Note: as you can see, this schedule is for many different kinds of income. Here I am writing about ONLY your income from master limited partnerships. If you have income from rental property, royalties, private partnerships, S corporations, trusts, estates, REMICs etc., they also go on this schedule. See your tax adviser.)

The biggest thing to remember about Schedule E is that, because it covers so many types of income — and we're only concerned with one — it's a lot more complicated than it needs to be for our purposes.

For reporting income from owning MLPs, you should ignore 95% of the Schedule E. Even the relevant 5% is just a fancy form for recording how much income you received from each MLP you owned and then adding it up. And then putting that total on your main tax form 1040.

For our MLP purposes, the rest of the form is just clutter. (Again, if you do have those other types of income, of course you must also complete the relevant portions of this Schedule E. See your tax adviser.)

Part I does not apply to this book.

Part II — With an MLP, you are not reporting a loss on this form because it does not reduce your other income, so check Line 27 "No."

On Line 28, fill in the names and employer identification numbers (from Part 1, block A of the K-1 forms) of all the MLPs you own.

In the B block, put a "P" for Partnership.

If you're a U.S. taxpayer and you own a U.S. MLP, it's NOT a foreign partnership so therefore do NOT check block (c).

All of your investment is at risk, so do NOT check block (e).

With MLPs, your income is non-passive, so ignore the Passive Income and Loss columns (f) and (g). You would report a loss in column (h) only if one is reported on the K-1. Remember that it does not reduce taxable income you may receive from any other source, including other MLPs.

(It's also possible to have both a loss and taxable income from the same MLP. You just have to look at the K-1. If it reports a loss as well as income, put that in Line 28 column (h).

The section 179 expense deduction from Form 4562 refers to calculating depreciation, which is the job of the partnership's tax return, so ignore column (i).

That leaves column (j). In this block, copy the amount of business income that's in Part III Line 1 of the K-1 form.

Write "From PTP" by the figure.

Add up all those amounts (one for each MLP you owned units of during the relevant calendar year) and record the total in Line 29a. Put the same figure on Line 30. Put it down again on Line 32.

Put that down again on Line 41, unless you have other Schedule E income.

Your Line 41 total goes on Line 17 of your 1040.

Ignore all the other sections and lines unless they apply to your individual situation. (They do NOT apply to ownership of MLPs. For everything else, see your tax adviser.)

That's it. Again, the bottom line is much simpler than the form makes it look.

You record each MLP you own.

You record your net income from each one.

(You cannot use losses on Master Limited Partnerships to reduce any income except income from the same Master Limited Partnership, so you can only add up the ones with net positive income.)

You add up the total.

You put the total on your 1040.

Note: by the way, many Master Limited Partnerships make your K-1 forms and information available online. They'll also import the information to Turbo Tax.

They also send you a complete package to walk you through the process.

Plus they have customer service representatives you can call for additional help.

The NAPTP link to tax info:

naptp.org/Navigation/InvestorRelations/IRtax/IRResources_Main.htm

And if you think all this is bad, just read what non-U.S. citizens or residents have to go through.

Chapter 17

If You are Not a U.S. Citizen and Not Residing in the United States

The United States government does not make it easy for you if you own MLP units.

When it comes to taxes, the United States government does not make it easy for ANYBODY.

If you own U.S. Master Limited Partnerships, the IRS has more paperwork for you, so it can make sure it collects any taxes you owe.

In 2010 continuing, the MLP must withhold money from your quarterly cash distributions to make sure your U.S. taxes are paid. You must obtain a taxpayer identification number from the U.S. Internal Revenue Service (IRS) and provide that number to the broker or other nominee receiving the quarterly distributions on your behalf on a Form W8-BEN to claim an income tax credit in your annual U.S. federal income tax return for the withholding taxes paid out of the quarterly distributions.

That is, the MLP is required by the IRS to withhold a certain amount of your quarterly distributions. You get credit for them only by filing the Form W8-BEN.

And apparently you have to file a U.S. federal tax return with the IRS. to get your money back.

All I can say is, don't think it's just because you're not in the U.S. — they are on our backs too.

It'd better for all of us if the United States would do away with all income taxes and adapt a national sales tax (or VAT), but that's not likely any time soon.

You should not owe any actual U.S. taxes unless the amount of taxable money you receive from MLPs inside the United States is large.

For more details, consult your tax adviser and local broker.

Chapter 18

How to Invest in MLPs in a Tax-Deferred Account or Just Avoid the Extra Paperwork

Although they don't take full advantage of the benefits of Master Limited Partnerships, there are four ways to tap into their cash flow inside your tax-deferred accounts or in your taxable accounts without creating extra paperwork at tax time.

If your only investment portfolio is a tax-deferred account, I do encourage you to use it to invest in MLPs in one or more of the ways listed below (more details in a later chapter), especially if you are more than five or six years left until retirement.

That is because, after you've recovered your initial cost basis through the "return of capital" portions of your quarterly cash distributions, all additional income is taxed at ordinary rates.

Therefore, beyond the first four to six years you own MLP units, it is a good idea to shelter your income from MLPs inside a tax-deferred account.

Take as much advantage of the cash flow from MLPs as you can.

If you are simply trying to avoid the extra paperwork of buying MLPs directly for a taxable account, I encourage you to use your extra income to hire an accountant to use Turbo Tax.

1. I-Units

2. Closed-End Funds

3. Exchange Traded Notes (ETN)

4. Buying shares of the corporations that control the MLPs.

Chapter 19

Master Limited Partnership I-Units

This method of investing in Master Limited Partnerships is good only for people who are not yet retired. If you need current income to pay your bills, this is not for you.

The only other drawback with this method is that it applies to only two Master Limited Partnerships. Therefore, there's not as diversification as I for one would like.

Fortunately, they're two of the oldest, most successful and highly regarded MLPs — Kinder Morgan and Enbridge Energy Partners.

They're called, variously, MLP I-Shares, IShares, and i-units.

The "i" stands for institutional. That's because i-units were created to encourage institutions to buy them despite their tax-free status. However, individuals also have the right to buy them, and probably most i-units are owned by individual investors.

Kinder Morgan and Enbridge Energy Partners both call them i-units, so I'll stick with that.

The actual, ordinary limited partnership units are generally called common units. That's one type of unit issued by the LP.

(They also offer a form of unit called Class B. Those carry voting rights and are not offered publicly. We're not concerned with them. But you may see references to them, and I'm trying to be as complete as possible.)

Kinder Morgan and Enbridge Energy Partners Also Offer I-Units

I-Units are actually ownership interests in a limited liability company which does nothing except own common units in the limited partnership.

Therefore, you gain control of the i-units by buying shares in the limited liability company, which you can do by giving your broker the buy order.

Master Limited Partnerships

You can buy shares in Kinder Morgan Management, LLC (NYSE: KMR).

You can buy shares in Enbridge Energy Management, L.L.C. (NYSE: EEQ).

When the MLP pays out a quarterly cash distribution to unit holders, owners of i-units receive the equivalent amount in the form of additional i-units.

They're therefore called paid-in-kind (PIK) securities. You get paid "in kind"— in additional i-units.

So, for example, if the cash distribution is $1 per unit and you own 100 i-units, you'll get $100 worth of new i-units. If the market price is $50 per i-unit, that's 2 additional i-units.

Next quarter, if the cash distribution is still $1 per unit, you'll receive $102 worth of new i-units.

Therefore, in effect, this works the same as a Dividend Re-Investment Program (DRIP). Your quarterly distribution is automatically reinvested into new shares.

That's why I said this is perfect for everyone who does not need current income to pay their bills. You should be reinvesting all your investment income into additional shares.

With i-units, Kinder Morgan and Enbridge Energy Partners are kind enough to do it for your automatically.

If you do this inside a regular brokerage account, you are liable to pay end of the year taxes on the value of the amount of dividends you received. This is true of DRIPs as well.

However, if you — like many people — have only a tax-deferred account to invest with, i-units are   perfect for you, except I'd prefer more choices for greater diversification.

When you do need to withdraw the money from your retirement account to begin receiving income to pay the bills with, you'll have to sell all those i-shares and buy whatever income investments are best for you at that time.

To obtain more diversification, we must look at closed-end funds.

Chapter 20

Closed-End Funds that Invest in Master Limited Partnerships

Open-end mutual funds, thanks to the 2004 American Jobs Creation Act, are allowed to invest in Master Limited Partnerships provided no more than 25% of their portfolio is in MLPs and they do not own any more than 10% of any one particular MLP.

Although designed to encourage mutual funds to buy MLP units, open-end mutual funds haven't shown much interest.

However, a few close-end mutual funds have decided to own MLPs.

They own a basket of MLP units, take a slice of the earnings to pay their management expenses, then pass the rest on to you in the form of taxable dividends.

Therefore, one drawback is that, although yields can be high because MLPs distribute a lot of cash, all the money you receive from the fund is taxed as ordinary income if you hold the shares inside a taxable account. You get a 1099 at the end of the year and must pay your taxes.

However, some people find this familiarity reassuring, and prefer it to accepting the tax advantages of owning MLP units directly in a taxable brokerage account.

You can also hold shares of these funds inside a tax-deferred account such as your traditional or Roth IRA.

But you do pay a price. Actually, three.

1. As mentioned, the dividends from closed end mutual funds are all taxable as dividends.

2. As mentioned, the fund management company takes a percentage as its management fee. This seems small, but can add up to a lot of money as the years go by.

3. Almost all these closed end MLP funds use leverage to "enhance" their returns.

This means that they borrow money to buy the MLP units. When they make money, they make more money.

But when they lose money — and although MLPs are in great businesses, there's no such thing as NO risk — they lose more money.

Here are the closed end mutual funds that invest in MLPs:

Cushing MLP Total Return Fund (SRV)

Energy Income & Growth (FEN)

Fiduciary/Claymore MLP (FMO)

Kayne Anderson Energy Development Company (KED)

Kayne Anderson MLP (KYN)

MLP & Strategic Equity Fund Inc (MTP)

Tortoise Capital Resources (TTO)

Tortoise Energy (TYY)

Tortoise Energy Infrastructure (TYG)

Tortoise North American Energy Corp. (TYN)

NOTE: Kayne Anderson also has another closed end fund, Kayne Anderson Energy Total (KYE), which also invests in MLPs. I'm not describing it in detail because it also invests in Canadian income trusts, U.S. royalty trusts, marine transportation companies, and coal companies.

Therefore, it's more a total energy play rather than an MLP only play.

Chapter 20-A

The Cushing MLP Total Return Fund (SRV)

SRV is managed by Swank Energy Income Advisers, LP, a wholly owned subsidiary of Swank Capital, LLC. Swank Capital launched one of the first MLP hedge funds in January 2003. Swank Capital is aligned with Riverstone Holdings, LLC, a private energy investment company.

SRV is a non-diversified, closed-end management investment company with an inception date of August 27, 2007. SRV invests in energy MLPs in the development, production, processing, refining, transportation, storage and marketing of natural resources. At least 80% of its holdings will be such MLPs. Up to 50% of its assets may be in private, restricted MLP securities. SRV currently pays $0.225 per quarter dividends. Its management fee is 1.25%. Leverage is 31.5%.

SRV Top 10 Holdings

Inergy LP
Markwest Energy Partners LP
Magellan Midstream Partners LP
Targa Resources Partners LP
Oneok Partners LP
Enterprise Products Partners LP
Regency Energy Partners LP
Boardwalk Pipeline Partners LP
Energy Transfer Equity LP
Plains All American Pipeline LP

NOTE: Swank also operates MLP hedge funds. I'm listing them here for the sake of covering all MLP-related investments as completely as possible. I don't recommend them on general principles because they're not liquid and they charge high management fees.

They're also not appropriate for most readers because — I'm assuming because they're hedge funds — they have high minimum investments.

Also, I believe the the hedge fund concept — which allows going short on securities as well as long — in flawed. It means the hedge fund manager must have dependable powers to predict the future.

Personally, I think you should just buy MLPs and hang on to them, cashing or reinvesting the quarterly distribution checks, for the rest of your life without ever thinking about shorting them.

Here's the list. If you're interested, contact Swank.

1. The Cushing MLP Opportunity Fund I, L.P.

2. Swank MLP Convergence Fund, L.P.

3. The Cushing Fund, L.P.

4. The Cushing GP Strategies Fund, L.P

SRV Composition by Sector

Natural Gas Gathering	20.00%
MLP General Partners	14.00%
Natural Gas Transportation	15.00%
Upstream	10.00%
Crude Oil Gathering/Transport	10.00%
Products Pipeline Storage	9.00%
MLP Bonds	7.00%
Propane	5.00%
Coal	5.00%
Shipping	5.00%

Website

swankfunds.com/our-fund.asp

Chapter 20-B

Energy Income & Growth Fund (FEN)

This fund's objective is to provide a high level of after-tax income by investing in the "cash-generating" securities of energy companies, with a focus on publicly traded Master Limited Partnerships and related entities in the energy field.

It invests "at least" 85% in securities of energy companies, energy sector MLPs and MLP-related entities. At least 65% of assets will be MLPs and MLP-related entities.

I'm not sure what "MLP-related entities" are, unless they're i-units from Kinder Morgan and Enbridge Energy and General Partners.

And there's some wiggle room for them to invest is other forms of securities.

The fund's adviser is First Trust Advisers, L.P. and sub-adviser is Energy Income Partners, LLC.

FEN pays dividends quarterly. As I write, it's paying $0.44 per quarter.

It's now trading at a slight premium to Net Asset Value (NAV), but that too could change.

(Although some financial experts advise you to never buy a closed end fund at a premium to NAV, I'm not certain that always applies. Because the underlying assets are not under your control, you cannot count on eventually receiving true value.

(It's quite possible to buy a closed-end fund at a discount to NAV — which seems nice — but then have the share price go down even more.)

The real problem with buying at a premium to NAV is that it lowers your "rightful" yield.

The fund's expense ratio (excluding current and deferred income taxes) is 3.32%. The leverage is 26.28%.

FEN Top Holdings

Magellan Midstream Partners, L.P.
Enterprise Products Partners, L.P.
Plains All American Pipeline, L.P.
Kinder Morgan Energy Partners, L.P.
Enterprise GP Holdings, L.P.
ONEOK Partners, L.P.
NuStar Energy, L.P.
Enbridge Energy Partners, L.P.
Energy Transfer Partners, L.P.
Sunoco Logistics Partners, L.P.

FEN Composition

Midstream Oil	46.8
Midstream Gas	37.1
Propane	6.1
Utility	5.4
Coal	2.4
Oil & Gas	2
Diversified Energy	0.2

The President is James A. Bowen.

According to their annual report, they also own shares in two Canadian income trusts —

Keyera Facilities Income Fund (Oil, Gas & Consumable Fuels sector)

Northland Power Income Fund (Independent Power Producers & Energy Traders sector)

They also own some energy-related common stocks. And they own some energy-related warrants.

They also write covered calls on their holdings, one form of using leverage.

Website

ftportfolios.com/Retail/cef/cefsummary.aspx?Ticker=FEN

Chapter 20-C

Fiduciary/Claymore MLP Opportunity Fund (FMO)

FMO states its objective is to generate cash income through investing at least 80% of its assets in MLP entities and at least 65% in equities of MLP entities. However, it may also invest in the stock of large cap companies in the real estate, natural resources and energy sectors. The fund's sub-adviser is Fiduciary Asset Management, LLC. Its expense ratio is 1.76% and its leverage ratio is 25.53%.

FMO Top Ten Holdings

Enterprise Products Partners LP
Kinder Morgan Management LLC
Inergy Holdings LP
Plains All American Pipeline LP
Enbridge Energy Partners LP
Magellan Midstream Partners LP
Oneok Partners LP
Boardwalk Pipeline Partners
DCP Midstream Partners LP
Williams Partners LP

FMO's Portfolio Composition

Midstream Energy Infrastructure Oil	35.40%
Midstream Energy Infrastructure Gas	25.70%
Gathering & Processing	11.90%
Propane	10.30%
Natural Gas Pipelines	9.30%
Upstream	4.20%
Coal	2.50%
Other	0.70%

FMO has a 30% portfolio turnover. Its current distributions are $0.335 per share.

Website

claymore.com/FMO

Chapter 20-D

Kayne Anderson Energy Development Company (KED)

KED is quite a bit different from the other closed-end MLP funds in that it puts more money into private Master Limited Partnerships than in publicly traded ones. Plus it invests substantially in the debt of energy companies.

Its inception date in September 20, 2006. Quarterly distribution is $0.30 per share as of March 2010.

Leverage, according to what I see on the annual report, is about 33%. Management and other fees are 2.4%.

KED Top 10 Holdings

International Resource Partners LP
Direct Fuels Partners LP
VantaCore Partners LP
Antero Resources Finance Corp.
Energy Future Holdings Corp
Enterprise Products Partners LP
Hilcorp Energy Company
Eagle Rock Energy Partners LP
Plains All American Pipeline LP
Dresser, Inc.

KED Composition

Private MLPs	47.00%
Public MLPs and affiliates	33.00%
Energy debt	20.00%

Website

kaynefunds.com/Ked.htm

Chapter 20-E

Kayne Anderson MLP Investment Company (KYN)

KYN's objective is to invest primarily in energy-related Master Limited Partnerships.

Its current quarterly per share distribution is $0.48.

KYN's Top 10 Holdings

Plains All American Pipeline, LP
Enterprise Products Partners, LP
Magellan Midstream Holdings, LP
Inergy, LP
Kinder Morgan Management, LLC
MarkWest Energy Partners, LP
Copano Energy, LLC
Energy Transfer Partners, LP
Energy Transfer Equity, LP
Enbridge Energy Partners, LP

KYN's Portfolio Composition

Midstream MLPs	71.00%
General Partners	8.00%
MLP affiliates	8.00%
Propane MLPS	7.00%
Shipping MLPs	4.00%
Upstream MLPs	1.00%
Coal MLPs and Other	1.00%

Their website does not give a straight leverage percentage. I had to look at the balance sheet. Ignoring preferred stock, I calculated a percentage of just over 20%.

The fund's expense ratio is also not clearly calculated for you. According to the expense ratio page, in 2009 management fees were 1.3%, other expenses were 0.3% and interest expense and auction agent fees were 1.5%. That's a total of 3.1% you pay to the fund.

Its website is —

kaynefunds.com/Kyn.php

Chapter 20-F

MLP & Strategic Equity Fund Inc (MTP)

MLP invests in publicly traded Master Limited Partnerships in the energy sector. This can include both domestic and international Master Limited Partnerships. It may also purchase MLP i-units.

MLP units and MLP i-units are considered MLP "entities," and MTP may invest in either one.

I can't figure out any reason for a closed-end fund to own MLP i-units instead of direct units, but I don't see any listed in the holdings so it's probably not an important issue.

It's managed by IQ Investment Advisers LLC, a wholly owned subsidiary of Bank of America. Fiduciary Asset Management is a sub-adviser.

Its inception date is Friday June 29, 2007.

It's currently selling at a 2.63% premium to Net Asset Value. However, this has fluctuated. Sometimes it sells at a slight discount to NAV. Its total expense ratio of 1.39%.

To "enhance its returns," MTP will enter into variable prepaid forward contracts. These forward contracts are to sell particular equity securities with terms of approximately one year. They buy the equity securities with the proceeds from the forward contracts.

A prepaid forward contract means that they're paid upfront to supply units in an MLP in a year's time, for a price that's determined now.

Say Generic MLP LP units are now selling for $50. Somebody pays the MTP fund $60 per unit right now to supply them with 100 units a year from now. The MLP takes that $60 per share, buys the units and pockets the difference. A year from now, it turns over the units to the buyer. If they're selling for below $60, MTP has a loss. If the units are now selling for over $60, the buyer has a gain and the MLP has a loss.

This is much like selling covered calls, only you're locked into the position.

In short, it's a form of gambling on the future fate of the unit market price.

Plus, they must pay taxes on their capital gains profits. I'd prefer to simply hold my MLP units until doomsday, never paying taxes on the capital gains.

However, they do say they have not been entering into forward contracts because of market conditions.

Also, unlike other closed end funds that own MLPs, MTP does not use leverage. I'm in favor of that. Leverage can increase returns but also increases risk.

Dividends are distributed every month, and that's a good thing.

In 2009 and so far in 2010, they paid out $0.07 per unit every month.

MTP Top 10 Holdings

Kinder Morgan Management, LLC
Plains All American Pipeline, LP
Enterprise Products Partners, LP
El Paso Pipeline Partners, LP
Boardwalk Pipeline Partners, LP
Magellan Midstream Partners, LP
Buckeye Partners, LP
ONEOK Partners, LP
Sunoco Logistics Partners, LP
Spectra Energy Partners, LP

Overall, their holdings have a bias toward what they call "higher quality" rather than higher market cap MLPs than the standard indices. And it's weighted more toward natural gas infrastructure and less toward oil and refined product infrastructure.

They are actively trading units. The first annual report lists a lot of types of securities that are not MLPs. The current one sticks to MLPs. However, their balance shifts over time.

Website

iqiafunds.com/fundsOverview.asp?symbol=MTP

Chapter 11-G

Tortoise Capital Resources (TTO)

TTO is a product of Tortoise Capital Advisers LLC. It invests primarily in private and microcap ($5 to $30 million dollars) public companies in the midstream and downstream energy infrastructure sector.

TTO invests at least 90% of assets in energy infrastructure companies, with at least 70% in qualifying assets.

TTO may invest up to 30% in non-qualifying assets which includes high yield bonds, bridge loans, distressed debt, commercial loans, private equity, securities of public companies or secondary market purchases.

Therefore, this fund deals with only small and therefore risky companies.

Of course, some of these companies will grow and become successful. Buying a fund such as this one is safer than picking and choosing such companies yourself.

But you're still investing more for future capital growth than for current income. Therefore, to my way of thinking, it's not worth the risk. The point of MLPs is to grab of piece of an ongoing stream of income that continues to grow.

If you buy a microcap stock and hope it will grow into a powerhouse in five or ten years, you're just putting off what you could be buying today from established MLPs.

And I certainly don't care to think about how up to 30% of assets could go to high yield (meaning "junk") bonds.

Anyway, that's my way of thinking. You're welcome to take a shot if you wish!

TTO's IPO was February 2, 2007. Its management fee is 1.50%.

Their quarterly distributions are $0.13 per share. Leverage is around 5%.

TTO Top 10 Holdings

High Sierra Energy, L.P.
Mowood, LLC

VantaCore Partners, L.P.
International Resource Partners, L.P.
Quest Midstream Partners, L.P.
Abraxas Petroleum Corporation
EV Energy Partners, L.P.
High Sierra Energy GP, LLC
LONESTAR Midstream Partners, LP
Eagle Rock Energy Partners, L.P.
LSMP GP, LP

TTO Composition by Sector

Midstream and Downstream	61.00%
Aggregate & Coal	32.00%
Upstream	7.00%

Website

tortoiseenergy.com/tto.cfm

Chapter 20-H

Tortoise Energy Capital Corporation (TYY)

TYY is run by Tortoise Capital Advisers. It began May 4, 2005.

Under "normal circumstances," TYY puts 80% of its assets into energy related securities and 80% into equity securities of Master Limited Partnerships and their affiliates in the energy infrastructure sector.

They may also invest up to 50% of their assets into "restricted" securities, which are illiquid. These can consist of MLP convertible subordinated units, MLP common units, and securities of private energy infrastructure companies.

Therefore, investors may benefit from access to investments they cannot own as ordinary investors.

They may invest up to 20% into debt securities, including "junk" bonds.

They may not invest more than 15% into any one security.

They do not engage in short sales.

From the information available, their leverage using bank debt and senior notes (not counting preferred stock) is around 14%.

According to their annual report, their target is 25% total leverage, including preferred stock. As of December 31, 2009 they had 27.7%.

The good news is that the turnover rate is only 14.86% and the management expense is only 0.95%.

As I write, quarterly dividends are $0.40 per share, but may be more or less when you read this.

Top Ten TYY Holdings

Enbridge Energy Partners, L.P.
Kinder Morgan Management, LLC
Sunoco Logistics Partners L.P.
Enterprise Products Partners L.P.

Master Limited Partnerships

Energy Transfer Partners, L.P.
Plains All American Pipeline, L.P.
NuStar Energy L.P.
TC PipeLines, LP   TCLP
Magellan Midstream Partners, L.P.
Boardwalk Pipeline Partners, LP

TYY Composition by Sector

Crude/Refined Products Pipelines	48.50%
Natural Gas/Natural Gas Liquids Pipelines	36.30%
Natural Gas Gathering/Processing	11.60%
Propane Distribution	3.20%
Shipping	0.40%

Website

tortoiseenergy.com/tyy.cfm

Chapter 20-I

Tortoise Energy Infrastructure Corp. (TYG)

TYG is another closed-end, non-diversified management investment company from Tortoise Capital Advisers L.L.C. investing in Master Limited Partnerships and their affiliates in the energy infrastructure sector. Its inception date was February 27, 2004.

TYG's mandate is to invest at least 90% of their assets in securities of energy infrastructure companies and at least 70% of total assets in units of MLPs.

They may invest up to 30% of assets into illiquid, restricted securities. These may consist of subordinated MLP units, MLP common units and securities in private energy infrastructure companies. Investments in private companies are limited to 5%.

They invest up to 25% of total assets in the debt of energy infrastructure companies, including below investment grade ("junk") bonds.

They will not invest more than 10% of total assets in any one security.

They will not engage is short sales.

Their turnover rate is 17.69%. Their management fee is 0.95%.

At the time of writing in March 2010, their quarterly distributions are $0.54.

TYG has $169,175,000 in senior notes. I can't determine an exact figure for leverage, but that seems high.

TYG Top Ten Holdings

Kinder Morgan Management, LLC
Enterprise Products Partners L.P.
Energy Transfer Partners, L.P.
Enbridge Energy Partners, L.P.
Inergy, L.P.
Magellan Midstream Partners, L.P.
Plains All American Pipeline, L.P.
Sunoco Logistics Partners, L.P.

Boardwalk Pipeline Partners, LP
TC PipeLines, L.P.

TYG Composition by Sector

Crude/Refined Products Pipelines	43.80%
Natural Gas/Natural Gas Liquids Pipelines	38.70%
Natural Gas Gathering/Processing	11.00%
Propane Distribution	6.10%
Shipping	0.40%

Website

tortoiseenergy.com/tyg.cfm

Chapter 21

Master Limited Partnership Exchange Traded Notes (ETN)

JPMorgan Alerian MLP Index Exchange Traded Notes (AMJ) were launched April 2009. They track the performance of the Alerian MLP Index (AMZ), and pay quarterly distributions. AMJ's management ("tracking") fee is 0.85%.

However, remember that exchange traded notes — despite their name — are NOT the same as exchange traded funds. This ETN is a senior, unsecured obligation of JPMorgan Chase & Co. You do have the additional credit risk that you would if you owned JPMorgan bonds.

With exchange traded funds (ETF), you the investor actually own a piece of a basket of financial securities or assets. If the ETF management company went out of business, you'd receive your share of the securities they owned.

However, with an ETN you own nothing but a promise from the issuing company. The issuing company doesn't own anything to back up its guarantee. The ETN issuing company is simply promising to pay you whatever the ETN underlying index eventually reaches. It's a promise to track the index.

Perhaps the first company to issue exchange traded notes for Master Limited Partnerships was Bear Stearns. In March 2008 Bear Stearns had to be bought out by JPMorgan, as part of the entire 2008 financial crisis that eventually saw other Wall Street giants either bankrupt, bought out or restructured.

Other ETNs (not related to MLPs but the principle is the same) were been issued by Lehman Brothers, which did go bankrupt in the September 2008 financial crisis. So the owners of those ETNs got the shaft.

Owners of Bear Stearns ETNs came close to that fate. Hopefully JPMorgan will never go bankrupt, but I can't predict the future. If you would own JPMorgan long-term bonds, there's no reason not to own these ETNs, because the credit risk is the same but the ETNs should pay a lot more money.

The maturity date is May 24, 2024. These notes will be closed out on or before that maturity date. Therefore, these ETNs are not an investment you can buy and hold, receiving cash payments for the rest of your life.

Website

careers.jpmorganchase.com/cm/cs?pagename=Chase/Href&urlname=jpmorgan/investbk/solutions/sp/etn#JPMorgan_Alerian

Chapter 22

Investing in the General Partners of MLPs

Some experts advise that the best way to invest in Master Limited Partnerships without the hassle of extra tax forms or through a tax-deferred retirement account is to buy shares in the General Partnership.

Most MLPs are closely associated with a larger energy corporation which used to own the pipelines and other energy infrastructure.

The MLP is basically controlled by the big corporation. And you can buy shares of the corporation's stock on the market.

This way, you receive some benefit from the cash flow of the MLP.

I cannot advise this strategy for several reasons.

First of all, the corporation is engaged in many other aspects of the energy business. They roll out their midstream operations into an MLP, then continue with their upstream and downstream activities.

These may or may not be profitable. Even if they are, they no doubt have a lot of fluctuation and volatility thanks to the market price of oil and natural gas. And to the success or failure of the corporation's business and other assets.

Secondly, the cash flow from the MLP may be just a small part of the corporation's bigger picture. No matter how profitable the MLP pipelines may be, they likely won't amount to enough money to offset major losses in oil wells.

Thirdly, the corporation must pay income taxes. Avoiding taxation of corporate income is the main reason why MLP are such wonderful cash cows.

But once the cash reaches the corporation, the corporation must pay taxes (current corporate tax rate in the United States is 35%, but that could change) on that money.

Suddenly it's in the hands of the IRS, not available for distribution to shareholders.

Fourthly, the corporation is under no obligation to send out 90% plus of its cash to shareholders, as MLPs are.

They're under no obligation to pay quarterly dividends at all.

If they do, 50% is about the highest payout percentage you're likely to see. Many don't pay that much, especially corporations that need to spend a lot of money on new equipment, such as energy related companies.

Therefore, if you invest in the shares of a corporation that controls an MLP, you'll get a very diluted cash income from the MLP — and maybe none at all.

Chapter 23

Guidelines for Investing in MLPs

As I've stated before, to benefit from the full power of Master Limited Partnerships, buy their units in a taxable brokerage account and never sell them.

MLPs in a Taxable Account

To use diversification to reduce your risk, spread your purchases among as many MLPs as you can — at least 10.

I realize that's a lot of money and not everybody can buy 100 units of ten different MLPs at one time — me included.

So buy 100 shares of one now. When you have the cash (from your job, business or from income accumulated in your broker account), buy 100 shares of another one.

And so on.

Pick one of the MLP indexes. Use Alerian, S&P, Citigroup, Cushing, Tortoise, or Wells Fargo. Your choice.

Buy the first MLP on their list. Then the second. And so on.

In time, you create your own "index fund."

MLPs in a Tax-Deferred Account or If You Refuse to Deal With the Paperwork Connected With a Taxable Account

My suggestion is to never buy MLP units within a tax-deferred account. You're not only losing the tax benefits, you're risking a lot of hassle and expense from your account custodian.

However, it is a good idea to receive -- and shelter -- cash flow from MLPs inside a taxable account.

You have three imperfect but reasonable choices.

I-Units

Buy i-units in Kinder Morgan Management, LLC (NYSE: KMR) and/or Enbridge Energy Management, L.L.C. (NYSE: EEQ).

In lieu of cash, you will receive quarterly distributions of additional units.

In effect, they are automatic reinvestment programs. Every quarter the number of i-units you receive will go up.

I-Units cost about the same as the equivalent common units, so whenever you start making withdrawals from this account, you'll get the same amount of money from them as cash.

The biggest disadvantage is that only the above two MLPs offer i-units, so your account's MLP fate is tied to them.

The good news is that they're universally recognized as two of the best MLPs in existence.

Closed-End MLP Funds

There are some closed-end funds that invest mainly in Master Limited Partnerships. I've included more detail on them all in previous chapters.

The chief advantage is that the closed end funds are automatically more diversified than buying i-units in just two companies.

There are disadvantages:

1. Management fees.

2. Use of leverage.

3. In the case of MLP & Strategic Equity Fund Inc (MTP), use of forward contracts — not leverage.

Two aspects of closed-end funds can cut both ways.

They don't sell at Net Asset Value. If they're selling at a discount to NAV, you obtain extra yield.

However, if they're selling at a premium to NAV, you get a reduced yield.

And some of them invest in private Master Limited Partnerships. These are companies NOT publicly listed. Ordinary investors do not have access to these.

But they're risky.

If they work out as planned, they can return a lot of money.

But they're more likely to bomb than ordinary MLPs.

To diversify risk, I suggest going with one of the leveraged-closed end funds, especially one that focuses on publicly traded MLPS, and MLP & Strategic Equity Fund Inc (MTP).

Exchange Traded Notes

Exchange Traded Notes (ETN) from JPMorgan track the return of the Alerian MLP Index, but are like buying bonds in JPMorgan. If that firm ever goes down the tubes, so will their ETNs.

There are no perfect choices here. Everything is a trade off.

I suggest that you buy i-units in both of the companies offering them, one leveraged closed-end fund (perhaps the one with the highest discount to NAV — or lowest premium to NAV) and — if you're willing to take the risk (the same as buying JPMorgan long-term bonds — a smaller amount of money in ECNs.

Chapter 24

MLPs and the Remainder of Your Portfolio

I'm a big fan of diversifying your portfolio, but not of allocation percentages and certainly not of reallocating assets.

I don't believe anybody has figured out an optimal allocation percentage for capital gains investing, let alone for income investing.

They use historical figures of price volatility to determine the "risk" of each investment, then decide how to balance them depending on how much "risk" you say (or your broker decides for you, as my mother's former broker did) you're willing to accept.

Besides, historical returns do not guarantee future results — no government agency ever spoke truer words than these. But Wall Street routinely ignores them when managing funds and portfolios.

And nobody knows the true chances of each type of income investment's payouts going up or down in the future.

And when one of your investments does well, asset allocators want you to sell some of it to "reduce" your risk. But that's really forcing you to pay another broker commission and capital gains taxes to Uncle Sam (in taxable accounts).

(Besides, over the long run portfolio with various asset classes should balance themselves — because different asset classes will do better than others during different time periods.)

Master Limited Partnerships

I believe that Master Limited Partnerships are the best single type of investment available today to ordinary investors.

However, as an advocate of "safety through diversification," I don't advise you to place only MLPs in your portfolio — taxable or tax-deferred.

What if somebody actually did that and two years from now the federal government passes a law forcing MLPs to pay taxes like a corporation?

I'm not saying that will ever happen, but I can't promise you it won't.

The future in unpredictable.

Therefore, you should never put all your eggs in one basket, even when it's the best basket available.

Diversify Your Portfolio Income

You should diversify with ordinary dividend paying stocks, utility stocks, real estate investment trusts, corporate bonds, municipal bonds (though not in tax-deferred accounts), Canadian income trusts, and government bonds.

And you should own them in both U.S.-based securities and international securities. (For more details, see my book Income Investing Secrets.)

If You Own Both Tax-Deferred and Taxable Accounts

A lot depends on their relative sizes.

If your IRA is your largest account and your ordinary broker account is small, buy as many MLPs as you can in your broker account and keep your other income-generating investments in your IRA.

If you're wealthy enough that your IRA is much smaller than your broker account, keep only other income-generating investments in your IRA. Buy MLPs in your broker account, but also keep it diversified.

These are my suggestions based on my opinions.

For more details regarding your personal situation, see your tax adviser.

Chapter 25

If You Insist on Selling MLP Units . . .

My general investing philosophy is to keep expenses as low as possible.

That includes brokerage commissions and taxes.

You have to pay brokerage commissions to buy securities. But you have to pay them to sell securities ONLY if you sell. If you never sell, you never have to pay a second commission.

And if you never sell, you don't have to pay taxes on capital gains.

This is especially important for Master Limited Partnership units because you receive a "return of capital" with every quarterly distribution check and that amount is taxable only if -- and only when -- you sell.

Therefore, by selling MLP units you're throwing away one of the biggest advantages of buying them in the first place.

Never sell, and you keep that cash in your pocket.

However, I realize that not everybody will listen to me.

Or the MLP you own could turn out to be a new name for Enron, or you're having a financial emergency, or something.

Your cost basis in the MLP units is whatever the total amount you paid for them was, including brokerage commissions.

Example of a Sale of an MLP

Let's say you just bought 100 units in XYZ LP for $49.50. That's $4950, and you paid a $50 commission (that's too high, you should be using a deep discount online brokerage, but I'm trying to keep the numbers simple). So your total cost basis is $5,000.

Every time you receive a "return on capital" in your quarterly distribution, that reduces your cost basis.

So, let's say that in the next two years you receive $2,000 in quarterly distributions that were "return of capital."

That makes your cost basis $3,000.

Now let's say you decide to sell.

The market price is now $60 per unit, so you get $6,000, and pay another $50 commission, so you receive a net of $5950.

Your total long term capital gain is $5,590 minus $3,000 equals $2,590.

However, because you received $2,000 through quarterly distributions, that is taxable as ordinary income, not at long term capital gains rates. That's one of the penalties for selling MLP units.

Don't say I didn't warn you.

However, the $590 you received on top of your original cost basis is taxed as a long term capital gain.

Save yourself all that trouble. Keep the MLP units and cash (or reinvest) the quarterly distributions checks for the rest of your life.

Chapter 26

MLPs in Your Estate

The old saying is that nothing is certain except death and taxes.

Thanks to the provision in the law that you don't have to pay taxes on the return of capital you receive in your quarterly cash distributions until you sell the units in a Master Limited Partnership, you can actually avoid paying those taxes forever — simply by not selling.

Eventually you will meet up with that other "certainty"— death.

At that time, your estate passes to your heirs.

The closing market price of the MLP units on your day of death becomes the cost basis for your heirs.

Therefore, if they're then foolish enough to sell those MLP units, they will pay capital gains taxes only market price increases after you've died.

You have not cheated death, but you have kept a lot of money out of the hands of the IRS.

My suggestion is to buy copies of this book for your heirs so that they'll appreciate — even before you pass away — what a wonderful inheritance you're providing.

And so they understand that they should NEVER sell the MLP units, but keep on receiving their ever-growing quarterly distribution checks.

If they're not yet retired, they'll be smart to reinvest that money into more MLP units.

Chapter 27

List of Master Limited Partnerships

The rest of this book consists of a list of energy and natural resource-related Master Limited Partnerships.

Double Triple Disclaimer

I am not listing any of these companies for the purposes of soliciting your investment. I am not a broker or financial adviser. I have no right to give you personal financial advice.

I am not recommending — or not recommending — any of these. It's simply a list.

I used the list on this web page run by the National Association of Publicly Traded Partnerships —

naptp.org/PTP101/CurrentPTPs.htm

I did not include the limited liability companies, companies based outside the United States, the limited liability company that's mislabeled on this page as a limited partnership, over the counter listings or any PTPs not connected with energy or natural resources.

I kept the companies in the categories determined by the NAPTP, but some of them are mixed. Many "midstream" MLPs are also involved in downstream activities. And many upstream MLPs are also involved in natural gas gathering and transport.

You are Responsible for Your Own Due Diligence

My descriptions in the "BASIC BUSINESS" sections give you a brief idea of what that company does. They are not meant to be a comprehensive analysis of the company's financial standing or entire range of business activities. If you really want to dig into a company's properties prospects, and their balance sheets and income statements, you must read their latest 10K report to the Securities and Exchange Commissions (SEC).

Most of this information could — and eventually will — change.

It's correct now, but may not be by the time you read these words.

Focus on the "Toll Booth" Master Limited Partnerships

However, it's fair to suggest that you invest only in the Master Limited Partnerships listed in the first section — "Pipelines and Other Midstream Operations, Compressing, Refining."

These are the "toll booth" MLPs that profit mainly from their volume of business without depending on the current price of a barrel of oil.

For the sake of making this book as complete as possible, I do also list the MLPs in the Propane & Heating Oil, Exploration & Production, Marine Transportation, and Natural Resources - Coal, Other Minerals, Timber sections.

However well-run these companies may or may not be, their businesses are riskier and their profits are subject to greater volatility.

I wrote this book for the "Toll Booth" MLPs. That's where I strongly suggest you focus your investment dollars.

Section One

Pipelines and Other Midstream Operations, Compressing, Refining

Atlas Pipeline Partners

NAME: Atlas Pipeline Partners, L.P.

STOCK TICKER SYMBOL: NYSE: APL

ADDRESS

1550 Coraopolis Heights Road
Moon Township, PA 15108

877-280-ATLS (2857)
FAX: 215-553-8455

K-1 FORMS: Available online and for Turbo Tax

IPO DATE: February 2000

CHAIRMAN: Edward E. Cohen

GENERAL PARTNER

Atlas Pipeline Partners GP, LLC

The GP is owned and operated by Atlas Pipeline Holdings, L.P. (NYSE: AHD).

BASIC BUSINESS

Transmits, gathers, and processes natural gas in the Mid-Continent (Oklahoma, Arkansas, Kansas and Texas) United States and the Appalachian Basin.

In the Mid-Continent they own and operate 9,100 miles of active gathering pipeline, 8 natural gas processing plants and 1 treatment facility. In the Appalachian Basin they formed a joint venture with the Williams Companies — Laurel Mountain Midstream, LLC. Laurel Mountain Midstream owns and operates over 1,800 miles of natural gas gathering pipelines with over 7,400 wells connected.

WEBSITE

atlaspipelinepartners.com/overview.html

Atlas Pipeline Holdings

NAME: Atlas Pipeline Holdings, L.P.

STOCK TICKER SYMBOL: NYSE: AHD

ADDRESS

1845 Walnut Street
Suite 1000
Philadelphia, PA 19103

877·280·ATLS (2857)
FAX: 215·553·8455

K-1 FORMS: Available online and for Turbo Tax

IPO DATE: September 13, 2006

GENERAL PARTNER

Atlas America, Inc.

CHAIRMAN OF THE BOARD: Edward E. Cohen

BASIC BUSINESS

AHD 100% owns Atlas Pipeline Partners GP, LLC, which is the GP of Atlas Pipeline Partners.

WEBSITE

atlaspipelineholdings.com/

Boardwalk Pipeline Partners

NAME: Boardwalk Pipeline Partners, L.P.

STOCK TICKER SYMBOL: NYSE: BWP

ADDRESS

9 Greenway Plaza, Suite 2800
Houston, TX 77046
(713) 479-8000

K-1 FORMS: Available online and for Turbo Tax

IPO DATE: November 15, 2005

GENERAL PARTNER

Boardwalk GP, LP

Which is 100% owned by Loew's Corporation

CEO, PRESIDENT AND DIRECTOR: Rolf A. Gafvert

BASIC BUSINESS

The interstate transportation and storage of natural gas.

Boardwalk owns three interstate natural gas pipeline systems through three separate subsidiaries carrying 4.8 billion cubic feet (Bcf) daily. Together they have about 14,200 miles of pipeline and underground storage fields with aggregate working gas capacity of approximately 163 Bcf.

That's 8% of America's average daily consumption of natural gas.

Gulf South Pipeline gathers gas from basins between Texas and Alabama and delivers it to nearby markets and to the Northeast and Southeast.

Texas Gas Transmission is a "long-haul" pipeline moving gas from Gulf Coast supply areas to the Midwest and Northeast.

Gulf Crossing Pipeline Company LLC, operates the new Gulf Crossing interstate pipeline. It began operating in the first quarter of 2009. Gulf Crossing goes from Sherman, Texas to Perryville Louisiana.

WEBSITE

boardwalkpipelines.com/default.aspx

Buckeye Partners

NAME: Buckeye Partners, L.P.

STOCK TICKER SYMBOL: NYSE: BPL

ADDRESS

One Greenway Plaza
Suite 600
Houston, TX 77046
1-800-422-2825

K-1 FORMS: Available online and for Turbo Tax

IPO DATE: 1986

GENERAL PARTNER

Buckeye GP LLC

Which is owned and controlled by Buckeye GP Holdings L.P.

CHAIRMAN AND CHIEF EXECUTIVE OFFICER: Forrest E. Wylie

BASIC BUSINESS

Midstream energy logistics — large independent pipeline 5,400 mile long network carrying refined petroleum products including gasoline, jet fuel, diesel fuel, heating oil and kerosene. It also owns 64 refined petroleum terminals with storage capacity of 24 million barrels. Owns subsidiary Farm & Home Oil Company which is a leading independent fuel distributor in Mid-Atlantic region.

BPL also is the largest stockholder of West Shore Pipe Line Company. It owns a 20% interest in West Texas LPG Pipeline, LP and 75% of WesPac Pipelines-Memphis LLC. Subsidiary Lodi Gas Storage owns and operates natural gas storage facilities with approximately 22 billion cubic feet ("Bcf") of capacity in northern California.

WEBSITE

buckeye.com/

Buckeye GP Holdings

NAME: Buckeye GP Holdings, L.P.

STOCK TICKER SYMBOL: NYSE: BGH

ADDRESS

One Greenway Plaza
Suite 600
Houston, TX 77046 77046

K-1 FORMS: Available online and for Turbo Tax

IPO DATE: August 9, 2006

GENERAL PARTNER

MainLine Management LLC

Which is 100% owned by BGH GP Holdings, LLC.

Which is owned by affiliates of ArcLight Capital Partners, LLC, Kelso & Company, certain investment funds and some members of senior management

CHAIRMAN OF THE BOARD

They do not have any officers or directors. Mainline Management handles all that.

Mainline Management's Chairman of the Board, CEO and Director: Forest E. Wylie

BASIC BUSINESS

Owns Buckeye GP LLC, which is the General Partner for Buckeye Partners, L.P. Therefore, it receives the benefit of the incentive distributions rights it receives.

WEBSITE

buckeyegp.com/

Calumet Specialty Products Partners

NAME: Calumet Specialty Products Partners, L.P.

STOCK TICKER SYMBOL: NASDAQ: CLMT

ADDRESS

2780 Waterfront Pkwy E. Drive, Suite 200
Indianapolis, Indiana 46214
(317) 328-5660

K-1 FORMS: Available online and for Turbo Tax

IPO DATE: January 31, 2006

GENERAL PARTNER

CALUMET GP, LLC

CHAIRMAN OF THE BOARD

Chairman of the Board of the GP: Fred M. Fehsenfeld, Jr.

BASIC BUSINESS

Leading refiner and processor of specialty hydrocarbon products. Calumet has the most diverse specialty hydrocarbon capability in the world.

Products include naphthenic and paraffinic oils, aliphatic solvents, white mineral oils, petroleum waxes, petrolatum and hydrocarbon gels. Operates plants including operations in Northwest Louisiana (Princeton, Cotton Valley and Shreveport), Karns City Pennsylvania, Burnham Illinois and Dickenson Texas.

Owns Burnham Illinois terminal containing a manufacturing and bulk storage facility with over six million gallons capacity for tank truck delivery throughout the upper Midwest.

WEBSITE

calumetspecialty.com/

Cheniere Energy Partners

NAME: Cheniere Energy Partners, L.P.

STOCK TICKER SYMBOL: NYSE EuroNext: CQP

ADDRESS

700 Milam Street, Suite 800
Houston, Texas 77002

(713) 375-5000
FAX: (713) 375-6000

K-1 FORMS: Available online and for Turbo Tax

IPO DATE: 2007

GENERAL PARTNER

Cheniere Energy, Inc.

CHAIRMAN OF THE BOARD OF DIRECTORS OF THE COMPANY, AND
CHIEF EXECUTIVE OFFICER AND PRESIDENT: Charif Souki

BASIC BUSINESS

Formed to develop, own and operate the Sabine Pass LNG receiving terminal in
western Cameron Parish, Louisiana on the Sabine Pass Channel. It's under
construction.

The Sabine Pass LNG terminal is located on 853 acres of land along the Sabine
Pass River on the border between Texas and Louisiana, in Cameron Parish,
Louisiana.

Owns Sabine Pass LNG, L.P.

WEBSITE

cheniereenergypartners.com/

Crosstex Energy

NAME: Crosstex Energy, L.P.

STOCK TICKER SYMBOL: NASDAQ: XTEX

ADDRESS:

2501 Cedar Springs Suite 100
Dallas, Texas 75201

(214) 953-9500

K-1 FORMS: Available online and for Turbo Tax

IPO DATE: 1996

GENERAL PARTNER

Crosstex Energy GP, L.P.

Which is owned by Crosstex Energy, Inc.

CHAIRMAN OF THE BOARD: Rhys J. Best

BASIC BUSINESS

Gas gathering, processing, transmission, distribution, supply and marketing, as well as crude oil and natural gas liquids (NGL) marketing. Owns over 3,300 miles of natural gas pipeline. Owns 10 gas processing plants and 3 fractionation facilities. It transports over 3.2 billion cubic feet per day.

XTEX fractionates processed gas into natural gas liquid components (propane, butane, and others). They also separate CO_2 and recover sulfur.

WEBSITE

crosstexenergy.com/

DCP Midstream Partners

NAME: DCP Midstream Partners, L.P

STOCK TICKER SYMBOL: NYSE: DPM

ADDRESS

370 17th Street
Suite 2775
Denver, CO 80202
(303) 633-2900

K-1 FORMS: Available online and for Turbo Tax

IPO DATE: December 2, 2005

GENERAL PARTNER

DCP Midstream GP, LLC

Which is operated by its General Partner DCP Midstream, LLC but 99% owned by Limited Partner DCP Midstream, LLC.

Which is owned by Spectra Energy and ConocoPhillips.

CHAIRMAN: Thomas C. O'Connor

BASIC BUSINESS

Gathers, treats, processes, transports, and markets natural gas and natural gas liquids (NGLs) and is a leading wholesale distributor of propane.

Their operations are organized into three business segments, Natural Gas Services and NGL Logistics and Wholesale Propane Logistics.

Natural gas — Interests in Collbran Gas Gathering; Antrim Gathering; DCP East Texas Holdings, LLC; Discovery Producer Services, LLC; Douglas Gas Gathering; and Michigan Systems. NGL Logistics — Seabreeze Pipeline, Wilbreeze Pipeline and Black Lake Pipeline.

Wholesale Propane — Gas Supply Resources which owns six rail and one pipeline terminal, one leased marine terminal, and use of several open-access pipeline terminals. Aggregate storage capacity of approximately 475 MBbls.

WEBSITE

dcppartners.com/Pages/Home.aspx

Duncan Energy Partners

NAME: Duncan Energy Partners, L.P.

STOCK TICKER SYMBOL: NYSE: DEP

ADDRESS

1100 Louisiana Street
10th floor
Houston, TX 77002

P.O. Box 4324
Houston, TX 77210 - 4324

Main: (713) 381-6500
Investors: (713) 381-6812

K-1 FORMS: Available online

IPO DATE: February 5, 2007

GENERAL PARTNER

DEP Holdings, LLC

Which is owned by Enterprise Products Partners L.P.

CHAIRMAN: Dan L. Duncan

BASIC BUSINESS

DEP provides midstream energy services. This includes gathering, transportation, marketing and storage of natural gas, and NGL fractionation (or separation), transportation and storage, and petrochemical transportation and storage. And they offshore production platform services.

DEP owns interests in assets primarily in Texas and Louisiana. This includes interests in 9,200 miles of natural gas pipelines with a capacity of 6.8 billion cubic feet ("Bcf") per day. They own more than 1,600 miles of NGL and petrochemical pipelines including access to the world's largest fractionation complex at Mont Belvieu, Texas. They have two NGL fractionation facilities in south Texas. 18 million barrels ("MMBbls") of leased NGL storage capacity. 8.5

Bcf of leased natural gas storage capacity. 34 underground salt dome caverns at Mont Belvieu with more than 100 MMBbls of NGL storage capacity.

WEBSITE

deplp.com/

Eagle Rock Energy Partners

NAME: Eagle Rock Energy Partners, L.P.

STOCK TICKER SYMBOL: NASDAQ: EROC

ADDRESS

Eagle Rock Energy Partners, L.P.
1415 Louisiana, Suite 2700
Houston, Texas 77002

(281) 408-1200

K-1 FORMS: Available online

IPO DATE: October 25, 2006

GENERAL PARTNER

Eagle Rock Energy GP, L.P.

Its GP is Eagle Rock Energy G&P, LLC.

CHAIRMAN AND CHIEF EXECUTIVE OFFICER: Joseph A. Mills

BASIC BUSINESS

EROC operates in midstream, upstream and mineral sectors.

EROC is involved with gathering, compressing, treating, processing and transporting natural gas; fractionating and transporting natural gas liquids (NGLs); and marketing natural gas, condensate and NGLs. It has natural gas assets in the Texas Panhandle, South Texas, East Texas and Louisiana.

EROC also owns upstream companies Escambia Asset Corporation, Redman Energy and Stanolind Oil and Gas Corp. EROC engages in low-risk development drilling — not high-risk exploration projects. It owns 157 gross productive wells.

Not typical of MLPs, EROC owns fee mineral, royalty and overriding royalty interests. These interests do not bear drilling or production costs. Their ownership may be perpetual. Also, they have the potential for "regeneration".

These are in 2,500 productive wells — 430,000 net mineral acres in 13 basins across 17 states.

WEBSITE

eaglerockenergy.com/

El Paso Pipeline Partners

NAME: El Paso Pipeline Partners, L.P.

STOCK TICKER SYMBOL: NYSE: EPB

ADDRESS

1001 Louisiana Street
Houston, TX 77002
PO Box 2511
Houston, TX 77252-2511

713.420.2600

K-1 FORMS: Available online and for Turbo Tax

IPO DATE: November 2007

GENERAL PARTNER

El Paso Pipeline GP Company, L.L.C.

Which is owned by the El Paso Corporation

CHAIRMAN OF THE BOARD of the El Paso Pipeline GP Company, L.L.C.: Ronald L. Kuehn Jr.

BASIC BUSINESS

Owns (directly or through subsidiaries) subsidiaries El Paso Pipeline Partners Operating Company, L.L.C.; W.I.C. Holdings Company, L.L.C.; El Paso Wyoming Gas Supply Company, L.L.C.; EPP SNG GP Holdings, L.L.C.; EPP CIG GP Holdings, L.L.C.; and Wyoming Interstate Company Ltd.

Through these subsidiaries, owns and operates natural gas transportation pipelines and storage assets.

Wyoming Interstate, Colorado Interstate Gas, Southern Natural Gas.

Muldon and Bear Creek storage facilities. Four storage fields in Colorado and Kansas.

They are expanding with the CIG Raton Basin and SNG South System III.

WEBSITE

eppipelinepartners.com/

Enbridge Energy Partners

NAME: Enbridge Energy Partners, L.P.

STOCK TICKER SYMBOL: NYSE: EEP

ADDRESS:

U.S. Enbridge
1100 Louisiana St., Suite 3300
Houston, TX 77002-5217

(713) 821-2000
Fax: (713) 821-2230

World headquarters are in Calgary Alberta

K-1 FORMS: Available online and for Turbo Tax

IPO DATE: Not shown, but site info goes back to 1998

GENERAL PARTNER

Enbridge Energy Company, Inc.

Which is 27% owned by Enbridge, Inc.

Enbridge Energy Management, L.L.C. manages EEP

CHAIRMAN OF THE BOARDS: Martha O. Hesse

BASIC BUSINESS

World's longest crude oil and liquids pipeline system, running through Canada and the United States — 8,500 miles. It primarily takes crude oil and natural gas liquids from reserves in Western Canada to refineries in the U.S. The Lakehead System, the North Dakota System and the Mid-Continent System.

It owns subsidiaries in the Mid-Continent and Gulf Coast regions involved in natural gas gathering, transmission, processing, treating and marketing. Enbridge has interests in 12 transmission and gathering pipelines in six major pipeline corridors in Louisiana and Mississippi offshore waters of the Gulf of Mexico. These transport half of the Gulf of Mexico's deepwater production of natural gas. Enbridge Gas Distribution is Canada's largest distributor of natural gas. East Texas System, Anadarko System, and North Texas System.

WEBSITE

enbridgepartners.com/EEP/

SPECIAL NOTE

You can buy i-units of Enbridge Energy Management, L.L.C. (EEQ) which will pay you stock dividends equal to the amount of cash distributions paid by EEP.

This is a way you can benefit from an MLP in your tax-deferred account.

Or you can buy EEQ in a taxable brokerage account and not have to receive a K-1 form at the end of the year. However, the value of the stock dividends is taxable income.

This is, in effect, an automatic reinvestment of dividends and is good for anyone currently building their portfolio.

If you need current cash income, buy the common units of EEP.

Energy Transfer Partners

NAME: Energy Transfer Partners, L.P.

STOCK TICKER SYMBOL: NYSE: ETP

ADDRESS

3738 Oak Lawn Ave.
Dallas, TX 75219
(214) 981-0700
Fax: (214) 981-0703

K-1 FORMS: Available online and for Turbo Tax

IPO DATE: 1996

GENERAL PARTNER

Energy Transfer Partners GP, L.P.

Which is owned by Energy Transfer Equity, L.P. and managed by its GP Energy Transfer Partners, L.L.C.

CHIEF EXECUTIVE OFFICER AND CHAIRMAN OF THE BOARD: Kelcy L. Warren

BASIC BUSINESS

Owns and operates pipeline operations in Arizona, Colorado, Louisiana, New Mexico, and Utah. ETP owns the largest intrastate pipeline system in Texas. Through La Grange Acquisition, L.P., which conducts business under the assumed name of Energy Transfer Company ("ETC OLP").

Natural gas operations include gathering and transportation pipelines, treating and processing assets, and three storage facilities located in Texas.

Owns more than 17,500 miles of pipeline. These include:

Fayetteville Express Pipeline
Midcontinent Express Pipeline
ETC Tiger Pipeline

Energy Transfer Interstate Holdings, LLC ("ET Interstate"), ETC Fayetteville Express Pipeline, LLC ("ETC FEP") and ETC Tiger Pipeline, LLC ("ETC Tiger"). ET Interstate is the parent company of Transwestern Pipeline Company, LLC ("Transwestern") and ETC Midcontinent Express Pipeline, LLC ("ETC MEP").

ETP is one of the three largest retail marketers of propane in the United States. They have over one million customers through Heritage Operating, L.P. ("HOLP") and Titan Energy Partners, L.P. ("Titan").

WEBSITE

energytransfer.com/

Energy Transfer Equity

NAME: Energy Transfer Equity, L.P.

STOCK TICKER SYMBOL: NYSE: ETE

ADDRESS

3738 Oak Lawn Ave.
Dallas, TX 75219
(214) 981-0700
Fax: (214) 981-0703

K-1 FORMS: Available online and for Turbo Tax

IPO DATE: February 2006

GENERAL PARTNER

LE GP, LLC

CHIEF EXECUTIVE OFFICER AND CHAIRMAN OF THE BOARD: Kelcy L. Warren

BASIC BUSINESS

Owns Energy Transfer Partners GP, L.P., the GP of Energy Transfer Partners, L.P.

WEBSITE

energytransfer.com/default.aspx

Enterprise Products Partners

NAME: Enterprise Products Partners, L.P.

STOCK TICKER SYMBOL: NYSE: EPD

ADDRESS

1100 Louisiana Street
Houston, TX 77002

P.O. Box 4324
Houston, TX 77210-4324

(713) 381-6500 — Main
(866) 230-0745 — Investors

K-1 FORMS: Available online and for Turbo Tax

IPO DATE: July 1998

GENERAL PARTNER

Enterprise Products GP LLC

Which is 100% owned by Enterprise GP Holdings L.P. (NYSE: EPE)

(GP's incentive distribution rights are capped at 25%.)

CHAIRMAN: Dan L. Duncan

BASIC BUSINESS

Largest publicly traded energy partnership. Provides midstream services in natural gas, natural gas liquids, crude oil, refined products and petrochemicals. Owns 48,000 miles of onshore and offshore pipelines.

Services include: natural gas transportation, gathering, processing and storage; NGL fractionation, transportation, storage and import and export terminalling; crude oil and refined products storage, transportation and terminalling; offshore platform services; petrochemical transportation and services; and marine transportation services.

They link large supply basins in Canada, the United States and the Gulf of Mexico with consumers.

They own a salt dome for storage, 25 natural gas processing plants, 70 tow boats and 135 barges, 19 fractionation facilities, 6 offshore hub platforms, and the Houston Ship Channel Import and Export Terminals.

On October 29, 2009 Teppco Partners, LLC merged with a subsidiary of EPD.

WEBSITE

eprod.com/

Enterprise GP Holdings

NAME: Enterprise GP Holdings, L.P.

STOCK TICKER SYMBOL: NYSE: EPE

ADDRESS

1100 Louisiana Street
Houston, TX 77002

P.O. Box 4323
Houston, TX 77210-4323

713.381.6500 — Main
866.230.0745 — Investors

K-1 FORMS: Available online and for Turbo Tax

IPO DATE: August 24, 2005

GENERAL PARTNER

LE GP, LLC

CHAIRMAN: Dan L. Duncan

BASIC BUSINESS

Owns Enterprise Products GP LLC, the GP of Enterprise Products Partners, L.P.

It also owns uncontrolling interest in the GP of Energy Transfer Equity, L.P. and limited partnership interests in that same company.

WEBSITE

enterprisegp.com/index.html

Exterran Partners

NAME: Exterran Partners, L.P.

STOCK TICKER SYMBOL: NASDAQ: EXLP

ADDRESS

16666 Northchase Drive
Houston, TX 77060
281-836-7000

K-1 FORMS: Available online and for Turbo Tax

IPO DATE: October 17, 2006

GENERAL PARTNER

Exterran Holdings, Inc.

PRESIDENT AND CHIEF EXECUTIVE OFFICER: Ernie L. Danner

BASIC BUSINESS

Exterran Partners, L.P. provides natural gas contract operations services to U.S. customers.

WEBSITE

exterran.com/html/main.html

Genesis Energy, L.P.

NAME: Genesis Energy, L.P.

STOCK TICKER SYMBOL: NYSE EuroNext: GEL

ADDRESS

919 Milam, Ste. 2100
Houston, TX 77002
713-860-2500
713-860-2640 (Fax)

K-1 FORMS: Available online and for Turbo Tax

IPO DATE: December 1996

GENERAL PARTNER

Genesis Energy, LLC

Which is controlled by Denbury Resources Inc.

CHIEF EXECUTIVE OFFICER: Grant E. Sims

BASIC BUSINESS

GEL is in the midstream segment of the oil and gas industry in the Gulf Coast region of the United States, primarily Texas, Louisiana, Arkansas, Mississippi, Alabama and Florida.

Owns refinery-related plants, pipelines, storage tanks and terminals, barges, and trucks and truck terminals. Provides services to refinery owners; oil, natural gas and CO_2 producers; industrial and commercial enterprises that use CO_2 and other industrial gases.

Pipeline transportation of crude oil, CO_2 and natural gas. NEJD and Free State CO_2 pipelines.

Refinery services. Eight refining operations located predominantly in Texas, Louisiana and Arkansas. Refinery services involve processing high sulfur (or "sour") natural gas streams to remove the sulfur.

Supply and Logistics. Provides terminalling, blending, storing, marketing, gathering and transporting focused on crude oil and petroleum products, primarily fuel oil.

They own or lease over 280 trucks, 550 trailers and 1.1 million barrels of liquid storage capacity at eight different locations.

Owns 49% of DG Marine Transportation, LLC and its subsidiaries.

Industrial Gases. Supply CO2 to industrial customers.

Syngas -— Through a 50% interest in a joint venture — facility that manufactures high-pressure steam and syngas (a combination of carbon monoxide and hydrogen).

Owns Sandhill Group LLC – Processes raw CO2.

WEBSITE

genesiscrudeoil.com/

Holly Energy Partners

NAME: Holly Energy Partners, L.P.

STOCK TICKER SYMBOL: NYSE: HEP

ADDRESS

100 Crescent Court, Suite 1600
Dallas, Texas 75201

K-1 FORMS: Not available online

IPO DATE: July 8, 2004

GENERAL PARTNER

Holly Corporation

CHAIRMAN OF THE BOARD AND CHIEF EXECUTIVE OFFICER: Matthew P. Clifton

BASIC BUSINESS

1,500 miles of product pipelines transport light refined products from Holly Corporation's Navajo Refinery, Alon USA's Big Spring Refinery, and others in Texas, New Mexico, Arizona, Colorado, Utah, and northern Mexico. The products transported include conventional gasoline; federal, state, and local specification reformulated gasoline; low-octane gasoline for oxygenate blending; distillates that include low and ultra-low diesel and jet fuel.

Refined product terminals receive products from pipelines and Holly Corporation's Navajo and Woods Cross and Tulsa refineries, and Alon's Big Spring refinery. Terminals serve Holly Corporation's and Alon's marketing activities. Terminals also provide blending (to achieve specified grades of gasoline); storage and inventory management; and other services such as additive injection and jet fuel filtering.

WEBSITE

hollyenergy.com/

Kinder Morgan Energy Partners

NAME: Kinder Morgan Energy Partners, L.P.

STOCK TICKER SYMBOL: NYSE: KMP

ADDRESS

Kinder Morgan
500 Dallas St., Suite 1000
Houston, TX 77002
(713) 369-9000

K-1 FORMS: Available online and for Turbo Tax

IPO DATE: February 1997

GENERAL PARTNER

Kinder Morgan G.P., Inc.

Which is owned by Kinder Morgan, Inc.

CHAIRMAN AND CEO: Richard D. Kinder

BASIC BUSINESS

One of largest pipeline transportation and energy storage companies in North America. 37,000 miles of pipelines and 180 terminals. Transports, stores and handles energy products such as natural gas, refined petroleum products, crude oil, ethanol, coal and carbon dioxide (CO_2).

Largest publicly traded pipeline MLP.

Rockies Express Pipeline and Fayetteville Express Pipeline.

The largest independent transporter of refined petroleum products. One of the largest natural gas transporters and storage operators. The largest independent terminal operator. The largest transporter and marketer of CO_2. The largest handler of petroleum coke.

Kinder Morgan Canada operates the Trans Mountain pipeline, the Express and Platte pipelines, the Cochin pipeline, the Puget Sound and the Trans Mountain

Jet Fuel pipelines, the Westridge marine terminal, the Vancouver Wharves terminal in British Columbia and the North Forty terminal in Edmonton, Alberta. And the TMX – Anchor Loop Project.

WEBSITE

kindermorgan.com/

SPECIAL NOTE

You can buy i-units of Kinder Morgan Management, LLC (NYSE: KMR) which will pay you stock dividends equal to the amount of cash distributions paid by KMP.

This is a way you can benefit from an MLP in your tax-deferred account.

Or you can buy KMR in a taxable brokerage account and not have to receive a K-1 form at the end of the year. However, the value of the stock dividends is taxable income.

This is, in effect, an automatic reinvestment of dividends and is good for anyone currently building their portfolio.

If you need current cash income, buy the common units of KMP.

Magellan Midstream Partners

NAME: Magellan Midstream Partners, L.P.

STOCK TICKER SYMBOL: NYSE: MMP

ADDRESS

One Williams Center
Tulsa, OK 74172

(918) 574-7000

K-1 FORMS: Available online and for Turbo Tax

IPO DATE: February 2001

GENERAL PARTNER

Magellan GP, LLC

And MMP is the only MLP with no incentive distribution rights.

PRESIDENT AND CHIEF EXECUTIVE OFFICER: Don R. Wellendorf

BASIC BUSINESS

Own a 9,500-mile petroleum products pipeline system, including 51 petroleum products terminals.

7 petroleum products terminal facilities along the United States Gulf and East Coasts. 27 petroleum products terminals principally in the southeastern United States. An 1,100-mile ammonia pipeline system serving the mid-continent region of the United States

They own Longhorn Partners Pipeline, L.P.

WEBSITE

magellanlp.com/

MarkWest Energy Partners

NAME: MarkWest Energy Partners, L.P.

STOCK TICKER SYMBOL: NYSE EuroNext: MWE

ADDRESS

1515 Arapahoe Street
Tower 2, Suite 700
Denver, CO 80202-2126

Toll Free: (800) 730-8388
Office: (303) 925-9200
Fax: (303) 290-8769

K-1 FORMS: Available online and for Turbo Tax

IPO DATE: May 2002

GENERAL PARTNER

MarkWest Hydrocarbon, Inc.

CHAIRMAN, PRESIDENT AND CHIEF EXECUTIVE OFFICER: Frank M. Semple

BASIC BUSINESS

Gathering system and processing plant in East Texas. Gas gathering system and processing plant in Western Oklahoma. Gas gathering system and processing plant in Southeast Oklahoma. Twelve gas gathering systems and 4 lateral gas pipelines.

Franchise processing position in the Appalachian basin. Largest intrastate crude oil pipeline in Michigan.

Joint-venture with NGP Midstream and Resources to develop midstream infrastructure in the Marcellus shale.

Refinery off-gas processing, fractionation and transportation facilities.

Michigan Crude Pipeline, Hobbs NM Gas Pipeline and Arkoma Connector Pipeline.

MarkWest Liberty Midstream & Resources, L.L.C. and MarkWest Pioneer, L.L.C.

WEBSITE

markwest.com/

Nustar Energy

NAME: Nustar Energy, L.P.

STOCK TICKER SYMBOL: NYSE: NS

ADDRESS

2330 North Loop 1604 W
San Antonio, TX 78248
(800) 866-9060
(210) 918-2000

K-1 FORMS: Available online and for Turbo Tax

IPO DATE: April 16, 2001

GENERAL PARTNER

Riverwalk Logistics, L.P.

Which is owned by Riverwalk Holdings, LLC

Which is owned by NuStar GP Holdings, LLC

CHAIRMAN OF THE BOARD AND DIRECTOR: Bill Greehey

BASIC BUSINESS

One of the largest asphalt refiners. Operates petroleum product terminals and petroleum liquids pipelines. Owns 8,417 miles of pipeline, 82 terminal facilities, 2 asphalt refineries and 4 crude oil storage facilities. Assets are located in the U.S., the Netherlands Antilles, Canada, Mexico, the Netherlands and the United Kingdom. Owns asphalt refineries, refined product terminals, petroleum and specialty liquids storage and terminal operations, and crude oil storage tank facilities. A total of over 91 million barrels of storage capacity. Owns NuStar Logistics, LLP and NuStar Pipeline Operating Partnership, L.P.

WEBSITE

nustarenergy.com/Pages/default.aspx

ONEOK Partners

NAME: ONEOK Partners, L.P.

STOCK TICKER SYMBOL: NYSE: OKS

ADDRESS

100 West Fifth St.
PO Box 871
Tulsa OK 74102-0871

K-1 FORMS: Available online and for Turbo Tax

IPO DATE: 1996

GENERAL PARTNER

ONEOK Partners GP, L.L.C.

Which is owned by ONEOK, Inc.

PRESIDENT AND CHIEF EXECUTIVE OFFICER: John W. Gibson

BASIC BUSINESS

One of the largest publicly traded master limited partnerships.

Owns one of the nation's premier natural gas liquids (NGL) systems, connecting NGL supply in the Mid-Continent and Rocky Mountain regions with key market centers. Gathering, processing, storage and transportation of natural gas. One of the largest natural gas gathering systems.

Properties include: Overland Pass Pipeline, Arbuckle Pipeline, Guardian Pipeline Expansion and Extension, Grasslands processing and fractionating facilities in the Williston Basin of North Dakota, Fort Union Gas Gathering system, in the Powder River Basin of Wyoming.

Owns ONEOK Partners Intermediate Limited Partnership; Midwestern Gas Transmission Company; Viking Gas Transmission Company; Guardian Pipeline; OkTex Pipeline Company; ONEOK Gas Transportation; ONEOK Gas Gathering; ONEOK Gas Storage; ONEOK WesTex Transmission; ONEOK Texas Gas Storage;

Mid Continent Market Center; ONEOK Transmission Company; Bear Paw Energy; Crestone Energy Ventures; and ONEOK Services.

WEBSITE

oneokpartners.com/

Plains All American Pipeline

NAME: Plains All American Pipeline, L.P.

STOCK TICKER SYMBOL: NYSE: PAA

ADDRESS

333 Clay St.
Ste. 1600
Houston, TX 77002

K-1 FORMS: Available online and for Turbo Tax

IPO DATE: November 17, 1998

GENERAL PARTNER

PAA GP LLC

Which is owned by Plains AAP, L.P.

Which is managed and controlled by Plains All American GP LLC (it's their General Partner)

CHAIRMAN AND CEO: Greg L. Armstrong

BASIC BUSINESS

PAA is one of the largest independent midstream crude oil companies in North America. They own and operate 17,000 miles of crude oil and refined product pipelines, 85 million barrels of crude oil, refined products and LPG terminals and storage capacity and a full complement of truck transportation and injection assets.

8 million barrels of crude oil and LPG linefill in pipelines; 2 million barrels of crude oil and LPG linefill; 528 trucks and 631 trailers; and 1,697 railcars. Bluewater Gas Storage and Pine Prairie Energy Center.

WEBSITE

paalp.com/fw/main/default.asp

141

Quicksilver Gas Services

NAME: Quicksilver Gas Services, L.P.

STOCK TICKER SYMBOL: NYSE: KGS

ADDRESS

777 West Rosedale St.
Fort Worth, TX 76104
(817) 665-8620
Fax: (817) 665-5008

K-1 FORMS: Available online and for Turbo Tax

IPO DATE: 2004

GENERAL PARTNER

Quicksilver Gas Services GP LLC

Which is owned by Quicksilver Resources Inc.

CHAIRMAN OF THE BOARD: Glenn Darden

BASIC BUSINESS

Main asset is a pipeline system in southern portion of the Fort Worth Basin in north Texas, the Cowtown Pipeline. They gather and process natural gas from the Barnett Shale formation to extract natural gas liquids and deliver the residue gas.

KGS also owns a natural gas processing plant in Hood County, Texas, the Cowtown Plant. It's connected by the Cowtown Pipeline.

Owns Quicksilver Gas Services Operating LLC, Cowtown Pipeline Partners L.P., and Cowtown Gas Processing Partners, L.P.

WEBSITE

kgslp.com/

Regency Energy Partners

NAME: Regency Energy Partners LP

STOCK TICKER SYMBOL: NASDAQ: RGNC

ADDRESS

Suite 3700
2001 Bryan St
Dallas TX 75201

(214) 750-1771

K-1 FORMS: Available online and for Turbo Tax

IPO DATE: February 3, 2006

GENERAL PARTNER

Regency GP LP

Which as of June 18, 2007 is owned by an affiliate of GE Energy Financial Services, a business unit of General Electric.

And Regency GP LLC is the General Partner of Regency GP LP.

CHAIRMAN OF THE BOARD OF DIRECTORS, PRESIDENT AND CEO: Byron Kelley

BASIC BUSINESS

Specializes in the gathering and processing, contract compression, and transportation of natural gas and natural gas liquids. They are sellers of natural gas, natural gas liquids and condensate and do use hedging techniques to manage their risk.

Operates in Texas, Louisiana, Kansas, Arkansas and Oklahoma. Owns 5,950 miles of gas gathering pipeline, 767,060 horsepower of third-party compression, and 9 active processing and treating plants.

Frontstreet Hugoton LLC, CDM Resource Management and Nexus Gas Holdings LLC. Regency Gas Services LP. TexStar Field Services, L.P. 43% interest in the

RIGS Haynesville Joint Venture. Regency Intrastate Gas System (RIGS). Gulf States Transmission Corporation.

WEBSITE

regencygasservices.com/index.php

Spectra Energy Partners

NAME: Spectra Energy Partners, L.P.

STOCK TICKER SYMBOL: NYSE: SEP

ADDRESS

5400 Westheimer Court
Houston, Texas 77056.

K-1 FORMS: Available online and for Turbo Tax

IPO DATE: 2007

GENERAL PARTNER

Spectra Energy Partners GP, LLC

Which is owned by Spectra Energy Corp.

PRESIDENT AND CHIEF EXECUTIVE OFFICER: Gregory J. Rizzo

BASIC BUSINESS

Has ownership interest in properties in the Southeast: East Tennessee Natural Gas System, Saltville Gas Storage, Gulfstream Natural Gas System; Market Hub Partners; and Ozark Gas Transmissions.

This totals 3,100 miles of natural gas transmission and gathering pipeline and more than 49 Bcf of natural gas storage capacity.

WEBSITE

spectraenergypartners.com/

Sunoco Logistics Partners

NAME: Sunoco Logistics Partners, L.P.

STOCK TICKER SYMBOL: NYSE: SXL

ADDRESS

1 Fluor Daniel Drive
Sugar Land, TX 77478
281-637-6423

K-1 FORMS: Available online and for Turbo Tax

IPO DATE: February 8, 2002

GENERAL PARTNER

Sunoco Partners LLC

Which is owned by Sunoco, Inc and Sunoco, Inc. (R&M).

CHAIRMAN AND DIRECTOR: Lynn L. Elsenhans

BASIC BUSINESS

Acquires, owns and operates mix of crude oil and refined products pipelines, terminals and storage facilities.

Organized into three business units: Refined Products Pipeline System, Crude Oil Pipeline System, and Terminal Facilities.

Refined Products Pipeline System is 2,200 miles of refined product pipelines.

Crude Oil Pipeline System serves customers in Texas, Oklahoma and the Gulf Coast of the United States. 3,350 miles of crude oil trunk pipelines and 500 miles of crude oil gathering lines.

Terminal Facilities own and operate 42 inland refined products terminals with capacity of 10.1 million barrels. 23 million barrels of crude oil storage capacity, most at the Nederland Terminal in East Texas.

Fort Mifflin Terminal Complex, the Eagle Point Dock and the Marcus Hook Tank Farm.

WEBSITE

sunocologistics.com/

Targa Resources Partners

NAME: Targa Resources Partners, L.P.

STOCK TICKER SYMBOL: NASDAQ: NGLS

ADDRESS

Suite 4300
1000 Louisiana
Houston TX 77002

(713) 584-1000
FAX: (713) 584-1100

K-1 FORMS: not available online

IPO DATE: 2007

GENERAL PARTNER

Targa Resources GP LLC

Which is owned by Targa Resources, Inc.

CHIEF EXECUTIVE OFFICER: Rene R. Joyce

BASIC BUSINESS

Owns 3,950 miles of integrated gathering pipelines, 7 natural gas processing plants and a fractionator. Natural Gas Gathering and Processing Segment.

The Logistics Assets segment is gathering and storing mixed NGLs and fractionating, storing, treating and transporting finished NGLs. They are in Mont Belvieu and Galena Park, Texas and in western Louisiana.

WEBSITE

targaresources.com/index.html

TC Pipelines

NAME: TC Pipelines, L.P.

STOCK TICKER SYMBOL: NASDAQ: TCLP

ADDRESS

717 Texas Street
Suite #2400
Houston, TX 77002

K-1 FORMS: not available online

IPO DATE: 1998

GENERAL PARTNER

TC Pipelines GP, Inc.

Which is owned by TransCanada Corporation.

CHAIRMAN AND CHIEF EXECUTIVE OFFICER: Russ Girling

BASIC BUSINESS

Pipelines linking natural gas imported from Western Canada to the United States.

3,700 miles of federally regulated U.S. interstate natural gas pipelines

Great Lakes Gas Transmission LP, North Baja Pipeline LP, Northern Border Pipeline Company, Tuscarora Gas Transmission Company

WEBSITE

tcpipelineslp.com/

TransMontaigne Partners

NAME: TransMontaigne Partners, L.P.

STOCK TICKER SYMBOL: NYSE: TLP

ADDRESS

1670 Broadway, Suite 3100
Post Office Box 5660
Denver, CO 80217

303-626-8200
Fax: 303-626-8228

K-1 FORMS: Available online and for Turbo Tax

IPO DATE: March 9, 2005

GENERAL PARTNER

TransMontaigne GP L.L.C.

Which is owned by TransMontaigne Inc.

Which is owned by Morgan Stanley Capital Group Inc.

Which is owned by Morgan Stanley

CHIEF EXECUTIVE OFFICER: Charles L. Dunlap

BASIC BUSINESS

Owns and operates terminals and transportation operations along the Gulf Coast, in the Midwest, in Brownsville, Texas, along the Mississippi and Ohio Rivers and in the Southeastern United States. Provide integrated terminalling, storage, transportation and related services for the distribution and marketing of light refined petroleum products, heavy refined petroleum products, crude oil, chemicals, fertilizers and other liquid products.

Light refined products include gasoline, diesel fuels, heating oil and jet fuels. Heavy refined products include residual fuel oils and asphalt.

Facilities in five geographic regions.

Gulf Coast facilities consist of 8 refined product terminals, seven in Florida and 1 in Mobile, Alabama. 6.5 million barrels of storage capacity.

Midwest facilities a 67-mile interstate refined products pipeline between Missouri and Arkansas, the Razorback Pipeline, and 3 refined product terminals with 0.6 million barrels of storage capacity.

Brownsville, Texas terminal has 2.2 million barrels of storage capacity for liquefied petroleum gas, or LPG. Also operates a bi-directional refined products pipeline for an affiliate of Mexico's state-owned petroleum company to and from Brownsville and Reynosa and Cadereyta, Mexico. Also an LPG pipeline from our Brownsville facilities to our terminal in Matamoros, Mexico, the Diamondback pipeline.

River facilities are 12 refined product terminals along the Mississippi and Ohio Rivers with 2.7 million barrels of storage capacity. Also a dock facility in Baton Rouge, Louisiana that is connected to the Colonial Pipeline.

Southeast facilities 22 refined petroleum products terminals along the Colonial and Plantation pipelines in Alabama, Georgia, Mississippi, North Carolina, South Carolina and Virginia with storage capacity of 8.8 million barrels.

WEBSITE

transmontaignepartners.com/index_main.php

Western Gas Partners

NAME: Western Gas Partners, L.P.

STOCK TICKER SYMBOL: NYSE: WES

ADDRESS

1201 Lake Robbins Drive
P.O. Box 1330
Houston, TX 77251-1330

832-636-6000
832-636-6001 (fax)

K-1 FORMS: Available online and for Turbo Tax

IPO DATE: late 2007

GENERAL PARTNER

Western Gas Holdings, LLC

Which is owned indirectly by Anadarko Petroleum Corporation.

PRESIDENT AND CHIEF EXECUTIVE OFFICER: Donald R. Sinclair

BASIC BUSINESS

Provides natural gas services: gathering, compression, treating, processing and transportation in East Texas, West Texas, Mid-Continent and the Rocky Mountains.

They own 10 natural gas gathering systems, 6 treating facilities, 6 processing facilities, 1 FERC-regulated pipeline, 1 NGL Pipeline, 5,500 miles of pipeline and 215,000 horsepower of compression.

Dew Gathering System, Pinnacle Gas Treating, LLC, Haley Gathering System, Hugoton Gathering System, Chipeta System, Chipeta Processing LLC and NGL Pipeline.

They have contracted with Anadarko Petroleum Corporation to operate their assets and service their customers.

152

WEBSITE

westerngas.com/Home/Pages/Home.aspx

Williams Partners

NAME: Williams Partners, L.P.

STOCK TICKER SYMBOL: NYSE: WPZ

ADDRESS

One Williams Center 5000
Tulsa, OK 74172-0172

(918) 573-2078
(800) 600-3782

K-1 FORMS: Available online and for Turbo Tax

IPO DATE: February 2005

GENERAL PARTNER

Williams Partners LP GP LLC

Which is owned by The Williams Companies

CHAIRMAN OF THE BOARD AND CHIEF EXECUTIVE OFFICER: Steven J. Malcolm

BASIC BUSINESS

Natural gas transportation, gathering, treating, storage and processing. Natural gas liquid (NGL) fractionation. Oil transportation.

Owns interests in three major interstate natural gas pipelines that deliver 12 percent of the natural gas consumed in the United States — 12 billion cubic feet per day average.

Transco (100%) — 10,000 miles of pipeline from Texas to New York City.

Northwest Pipeline (65%) — 3,900 miles of pipeline from New Mexico to Canada.

Gulfstream Pipeline (24.5%) — 745 mile pipeline from Alabama to Florida.

Opal and Echo Springs processing plants in Wyoming.

Willow Creek processing plant in Western Colorado.

Four Corners system in New Mexico and Colorado.

Four processing trains on the Gulf Coast.

Mid-Continent Fractionation and Storage complex near Conway, Kansas.

Wamsutter LLC and Williams Four Corners LLC

WEBSITE

b2i.us/profiles/investor/fullpage.asp?f=1&BzID=1296&to=cp&Nav=0&LangID=1&s=0&ID=3639

Williams Pipeline Partners

NAME: Williams Pipeline Partners, L.P.

STOCK TICKER SYMBOL: NYSE: WMZ

ADDRESS

One Williams Center
Tulsa, OK 74172-0172

918-573-2000

K-1 FORMS: Available online and for Turbo Tax

IPO DATE: 2008

GENERAL PARTNER

Williams Pipeline GP LLC

Which is owned by The Williams Company

CHAIRMAN OF THE BOARD OF DIRECTORS AND CHIEF EXECUTIVE OFFICER: Steven J. Malcolm

BASIC BUSINESS

Created to own and operate natural gas transportation and storage. WMZ owns 35% of Northwest Pipeline GP.

This is a natural gas pipeline system from the San Juan Basin in New Mexico and Colorado through Utah, Wyoming, Idaho, Oregon, to Sumas Washington close to Canadian border. That's 3,900 miles. It's the only interstate natural gas pipeline going to the markets of Seattle WA, Portland OR and Boise ID.

WEBSITE

williamspipelinepartners.com/profiles/investor/fullpage.asp?f=1&BzID=1589&t o=cp&Nav=1&LangID=1&s=0&ID=7778

Section Two

Propane & Heating Oil

AmeriGas Partners

NAME: AmeriGas Partners L.P

STOCK TICKER SYMBOL: NYSE: APU

ADDRESS

460 North Gulph Road
King of Prussia, Pennsylvania 19406

(610) 337-7000

K-1 FORMS: Available online and for Turbo Tax

IPO DATE: April 19, 1995

GENERAL PARTNER

AmeriGas Propane, Inc

Which is owned by UGI Corporation

CHAIRMAN: Lon R. Greenberg

BASIC BUSINESS

Largest retail propane distributorship with 1.3 million residential, commercial, industrial, agricultural and motor fuel customers in all 50 states. One billion gallons of propane.

Also sells, installs and services propane appliances, including heating systems. Also installs and services propane fuel systems for motor vehicles.

Subsidiaries: AmeriGas Propane LP (AmeriGas OLP), AmeriGas Eagle Propane L.P. (Eagle OLP)

WEBSITE

amerigas.com/

Ferrellgas Partners

NAME: Ferrellgas Partners, L.P.

STOCK TICKER SYMBOL: NYSE: FGP

ADDRESS

7500 College Boulevard
Suite 1000
Overland Park, Kansas 66210

913-661-1500

K-1 FORMS: available online

IPO DATE: 1994

GENERAL PARTNER

Ferrellgas, Inc.

Which is owned by Ferrell Companies

CHAIRMAN OF THE BOARD

BASIC BUSINESS

Second largest retail dealer of propane and equipment and supplies in the U.S. One million residential, industrial, commercial, portable tank exchange, agricultural, and wholesale customers.

Two subsidiaries: Blue Rhino, Ferrellgas Partners Finance Corporation and Ferrellgas Finance Corporation

WEBSITE

ferrellgas.com/

Global Partners

NAME: Global Partners, L.P.

STOCK TICKER SYMBOL: NYSE: GLP

ADDRESS

800 South Street
Suite 200
P.O. Box 9161
Waltham, MA 02454-9161

781-894-8800

K-1 FORMS: Not available online

IPO DATE: September 29, 2005

GENERAL PARTNER

Global GP LLC

Which is owned by affiliates of the Slifka family.

PRESIDENT, CHIEF EXECUTIVE OFFICER AND DIRECTOR: Eric Slifka

BASIC BUSINESS

Storage, distribution, and marketing of gasoline distillates and residual oil. Owns, controls, and has access to one of the largest terminal networks of refined petroleum products in the Northeast. Total storage capacity of 9.3 million barrels.

Leading distributor of home heating oil, diesel fuel, residual oil, gasoline, and fuel additives in the Northeast U.S.

Products include: heating oil, gasoline, diesel fuel, residual fuels, marine fuels, bunkers, natural gas & electricity, public & private bids, risk management, biofuels, and premium fuels & additives.

Subsidiaries: Global Companies LLC and its subsidiary Glen Hes Corp, Global Montello Group Corp, Chelsea Sandwich LLC, and Global Energy Marketing LLC (Global Energy) and Global Operating LLC.

WEBSITE

globalp.com/index.cfm?nav=investors

Inergy

NAME: Inergy, L.P.

STOCK TICKER SYMBOL: NASDAQ: NRGY

ADDRESS

2 Brush Creek Blvd
Suite 200
Kansas City, MO 64112

877-446-3749
Fax 816.842.1904

K-1 FORMS: Available online and for Turbo Tax

IPO DATE: July 31, 2001

GENERAL PARTNER

Inergy Holdings, L.P.

PRESIDENT AND CHIEF EXECUTIVE OFFICER: John J. Sherman

BASIC BUSINESS

Retail marketing, sale and distribution of propane to residential, commercial, industrial and agricultural customers. Serves 800,000 retail customers. Also operates a 40 Bcf natural gas storage business; a liquid petroleum gas storage business; a solution-mining and salt production company; and a propane supply logistics, transportation and wholesale marketing business.

Fifth largest propane dealer in the U.S. It's the largest independent natural gas storage operator in the Northeast and has a natural gas liquids business in California.

Stagecoach Natural Gas Storage Facility, Steuben Natural Gas Storage Facility, Finger Lakes Liquid Petroleum Gas Storage Facility, Thomas Corners Natural Gas Storage Development, U.S. Salt Mining.

Marc 1 Hub line and North-South Projects in production.

Therefore, although classified as a "propane" MLP, it also gets significant revenue from midstream operations.

WEBSITE

inergylp.com/

Inergy Holdings

NAME: Inergy Holdings, L.P.

STOCK TICKER SYMBOL: NASDAQ: NRGP

ADDRESS

2 Brush Creek Blvd
Suite 200
Kansas City, MO 64112

877-446-3749
Fax 816.842.1904

K-1 FORMS: Available online and for Turbo Tax

IPO DATE: June 2005

GENERAL PARTNER

Inergy Holdings GP, LLC

PRESIDENT AND CHIEF EXECUTIVE OFFICER: John J. Sherman

BASIC BUSINESS

Is General Partner for Inergy, L.P.

WEBSITE

investor.inergyholdings.com/phoenix.zhtml?c=188318&p=irol-irhome

Star Gas Partners

NAME: Star Gas Partners, L.P.

STOCK TICKER SYMBOL: NYSE: SGU

ADDRESS

Clearwater House
2187 Atlantic Street
Stamford, CT 06902
(203) 328-7310

K-1 FORMS: Available online and for Turbo Tax

IPO DATE: December 20, 1995

GENERAL PARTNER

Kestrel Heat, LLC

Which is owned by Kestrel Energy Partners, LLC.

CHIEF EXECUTIVE OFFICER: Daniel P. Donovan

BASIC BUSINESS

Largest retail distributor of home heating oil. Serves 370,000 residential and commercial customers with oil and 7,000 propane customers.

Operates subsidiary Petro Holdings, Inc (Petro) and Star Gas Finance Company.

WEBSITE

star-gas.com/

Suburban Propane Partners

NAME: Suburban Propane Partners, L.P.

STOCK TICKER SYMBOL: NYSE: SPH

ADDRESS

P.O. Box 206
Whippany, New Jersey 07981-0206
973-503-9252

K-1 FORMS: Available online and for Turbo Tax

IPO DATE: 1996

GENERAL PARTNER

Suburban Energy Services Group LLC

PRESIDENT AND CHIEF EXECUTIVE OFFICER: Michael J. Dunn, Jr.

BASIC BUSINESS

Serves 1,000,000 residential, industrial, commercial and agricultural customers in 30 states. Sells propane, fuel oil and refined fuel. Fourth largest propane dealer in the U.S.

Agway Energy Services — natural gas and electricity to Pennsylvania and New York

Hometown Hearth and Grill — gas appliances such as barbecue grills

Suburban Cylinder Express — propane tanks

Also owns Suburban Propane LP, Suburban Sales and Service, Inc., Suburban Energy Finance Corporation

WEBSITE

suburbanpropane.com/

Section Three

Exploration & Production

BreitBurn Energy Partners

NAME: BreitBurn Energy Partners, L.P.

STOCK TICKER SYMBOL: NASDAQ: BBEP

ADDRESS

2187 Atlantic Street
Clearwater House
Stamford, CT 06902

203-328-7310
Fax: 203-328-7422

K-1 FORMS: Available online and for Turbo Tax

IPO DATE: October 10, 2006

GENERAL PARTNER

BreitBurn GP, LLC

CHAIRMAN OF THE BOARD OF DIRECTORS: Halbert S. Washburn

BASIC BUSINESS INFO

Oil and gas acquisition, exploitation and development.

Producing and non-producing crude oil and natural gas reserves located in the Antrim Shale in Michigan, the Los Angeles Basin in California, the Wind River and Big Horn Basins in central Wyoming, the Sunniland Trend in Florida, and the New Albany Shale in Indiana and Kentucky.

Lazy JL Field in Texas, limited partnership interest in a partnership that owns the East Coyote and Sawtelle fields in the Los Angeles Basin in California, transmission and gathering pipelines, three gas processing plants and four NGL recovery plants.

As of December 31, 2008, total estimated reserves were 103.6 MMBoe, 75 percent natural gas and 25 percent crude oil.

Santa Fe Springs Field

Rosecrans Field

East Coyote Field

Sawtelle Field

Antrim Shale

Prairie du Chien ("PRDC")

Richfield ("RCFD")

Detroit River Zone III ("DRRV")

Niagaran ("NGRN") pinnacle reefs

Black Mountain Field

Gebo Field

North Sunshine Field

Hidden Dome Field

Sheldon Dome Field

Rolff Lake Fields

West Oregon Basin

Half Moon Fields

Owns: BreitBurn Finance Corporation, BreitBurn Management Company LLC, and BreitBurn Operating, LLC,

WEBSITE

breitburn.com/

Dorchester Minerals

NAME: Dorchester Minerals, L.P.

STOCK TICKER SYMBOL: NYSE: NASDAQ: DMLP

ADDRESS

3838 Oaklawn
Suite 300
Dallas, Texas 75219

K-1 FORMS: Not available online.

IPO DATE: 2003

GENERAL PARTNER

Dorchester Minerals Management LP

CHIEF EXECUTIVE OFFICER: William Casey McManemin

BASIC BUSINESS

Owns mineral, royalty, and leasehold interests mainly of natural gas properties. Controls 3.1 million gross acres in 574 counties in 25 states.

Collects an override payment on the production of wells on the land it controls. Controls acreage in the Fayetteville Shale, Barnett Shale, Bakken/Williston Basin and in the Appalachians.

DMLP is forbidden from taking on long term debt.

WEBSITE

dmlp.net/

Encore Energy Partners

NAME: Encore Energy Partners, L.P.

STOCK TICKER SYMBOL: NYSE: ENP

ADDRESS

777 Main Street
Suite 1400
Fort Worth, TX 76102

(817) 877-9955
fax: (817) 877-1655

K-1 FORMS: Available online

IPO DATE: February 13, 2007

GENERAL PARTNER

Encore Energy Partners GP LLC

Which is "eventually" owned by Encore Acquisition Company

CHAIRMAN OF THE BOARD: I. Jon Brumley

BASIC BUSINESS

Formed to acquire, exploit and develop oil and natural gas properties in the Big Horn Basin in Wyoming and Montana, the Williston Basin in North Dakota and Montana, the Permian Basin in West Texas and New Mexico, and the Arkoma Basin in Arkansas and Oklahoma.

Their operating partner is Encore Energy Partners Operating LLC.

WEBSITE

encoreenp.com/

EV Energy Partners

NAME: EV Energy Partners, L.P.

STOCK TICKER SYMBOL: NASDAQ: EVEP

ADDRESS

1001 Fannin Street, Suite 800
Houston, TX 77002
713-651-1144
713-651-1260 - fax

K-1 FORMS: Available online and for Turbo Tax

IPO DATE: 2009

GENERAL PARTNER

EV Energy GP. L.P.

Which is run by its General Partner — EV Management, LLC

Which is a wholly owned subsidiary of EnerVest Ltd.

CHAIRMAN AND CEO: John B. Walker

BASIC BUSINESS

Focused on acquiring and operating oil and gas properties. Owns properties in the Appalachian Basin, the Monroe field in Louisiana Michigan, the Austin Chalk in South Central Texas, the Permian Basin, the San Juan Basin, and the Mid-Continent area.

Subsidiaries: EVPP GP LLC, EVCG GP LLC, EnerVest Production Partners, Ltd., EnerVest Monroe Gathering, Ltd., EnerVest Monroe Marketing, Ltd., CGAS Properties, L.P., EnerVest Cargas, Ltd., Lower Cargas Operating Company, LLC, and EV Energy Finance Corp.

WEBSITE

evenergypartners.com/

Legacy Reserves

NAME: Legacy Reserves LP

STOCK TICKER SYMBOL: NASDAQ: LGCY

ADDRESS

303 W. Wall St., Suite 1400
Midland, TX 79701

432-689-5200
Fax: 432-689-5299

K-1 FORMS: Available online and by Turbo Tax

IPO DATE: January 18, 2007

GENERAL PARTNER

Legacy Reserves GP, LLC

CHIEF EXECUTIVE OFFICER AND CHAIRMAN OF THE BOARD: Cary D. Brown

BASIC BUSINESS

Oil and natural gas operations in the Permian Basin and Mid-Continent regions, including these properties: Texas Panhandle Fields, Spraberry Field, Denton Field, East Binger Field, Farmer Field, Lea Field, and Langlie Mattix Field.

Subsidiary: Pantwist LLC.

WEBSITE

legacylp.com/

Pioneer Southwest Energy Partners

NAME: Pioneer Southwest Energy Partners, L.P.

STOCK TICKER SYMBOL: NYSE: PSE

ADDRESS

5205 N. O'Connor Blvd
Ste. 200
Irving, TX 75039

972-969-3586

K-1 FORMS: Available online and for Turbo Tax

IPO DATE: May 2008

GENERAL PARTNER

Pioneer Natural Resources GP LLC

Which is owned by Pioneer Natural Resources Company

CHAIRMAN AND CHIEF EXECUTIVE OFFICER: C.H. Rees III

BASIC BUSINESS

Owns oil and gas properties in the Spraberry field in the Permian Basin of West Texas. 1,100 identified producing wells in the Spraberry field with proved reserves of 23 MMBOE, 84% liquids and 16% gas.

Subsidiary: Pioneer Southwest LLC

WEBSITE

pioneersouthwest.com/

Quest Energy Partners

NAME: Quest Energy Partners, L.P.

STOCK TICKER SYMBOL: NASDAQ: QELP

ADDRESS

Oklahoma Tower
210 Park Avenue, Suite 2750
Oklahoma City, OK 73102

(405) 600.7704
(405) 600.7722 - fax

K-1 FORMS: Available online

IPO DATE: November 2007

GENERAL PARTNER

Quest Energy GP, LLC

Which is owned by Quest Resource Corporation

CHAIRMAN OF THE BOARD: Gary M. Pittman

BASIC BUSINESS

Oil and gas exploration and operation.

Cherokee Basin — six counties in southeastern Kansas and northeastern Oklahoma. More than 500,000 acres. Almost all reserves are CBM which is methane.

Also owns assets in Appalachian Basin and Seminole County Oklahoma.

WEBSITE

qelp.net/

Section Four

Marine Transportation

K-Sea Transportation Partners

NAME: K-Sea Transportation Partners, L.P.

STOCK TICKER SYMBOL: NYSE: KSP

ADDRESS

One Tower Center Blvd
East Brunswick, NJ 08816.

(732) 565-3818

K-1 FORMS: Available online and for Turbo Tax

IPO DATE: January 14, 2004

GENERAL PARTNER

K-Sea General Partner L.P.

PRESIDENT, CHIEF EXECUTIVE OFFICER: Timothy J. Casey

BASIC BUSINESS

Provider of marine transportation, distribution and logistics services. Operates fleet of tugs and tank barges serving major oil companies, oil traders and refiners.

Almost 30% of U.S. refined petroleum produced is delivered by water.

KSP has 66 tugboats and 77 barges operating in the Atlantic Ocean, the Gulf of Mexico, and the Pacific Ocean from Hawaii to Alaska.

WEBSITE

k-sea.com/

Martin Midstream Partners

NAME: Martin Midstream Partners, L.P.

STOCK TICKER SYMBOL: NASDAQ: MMLP

ADDRESS

4200 Stone Road
Kilgore, Texas 75662

903-983-6200
Fax: 903-983-6262

K-1 FORMS: Available online and for Turbo Tax

IPO DATE: 2002

GENERAL PARTNER

Martin Midstream GP LLC

Which is owned by Martin Resource Management Corporation

PRESIDENT AND CHIEF EXECUTIVE OFFICER: Ruben S. Martin

BASIC BUSINESS

Operates in the Gulf Coast area:

1. Terminal and storage services for petroleum products and by-products. 6 inland terminals and 17 marine terminals.

2. Natural gas gathering, processing and NGL distribution services through Prism Gas Systems I, L.P. and Woodlawn Pipeline Co., Inc. 658 miles gathering pipelines and a natural gas liquids pipeline.

3. Marine transportation services for petroleum products and by-products. 37 inland tank barges, 18 inland push boats, 4 offshore tug barge units.

4. Processing, manufacturing, marketing and distribution of sulfur and sulfur-based products produced by oil refineries.

178

WEBSITE

martinmidstream.com/

Teekay LNG Partners

NAME: Teekay LNG Partners, L.P.

STOCK TICKER SYMBOL: NYSE: TGP

ADDRESS

4th Floor
Belvedere Building
69 Pitts Bay Road
Hamilton, HM 08, Bermuda

K-1 FORMS: Not available online

IPO DATE: May 10, 2005

GENERAL PARTNER

Teekay GP L.L.C.

Which is owned by the Teekay Corporation

CHIEF EXECUTIVE OFFICER: Peter Evensen

BASIC BUSINESS

Transporting natural gas to end user. Must be liquified into liquified natural gas (LNG) to 1/600 its volume and kept cyrogenically at a very low temperature.

LNG/LPG fleet — 14 LNG carrier and 3 LPG carrier tankers (3 on order) — many double-hulled

Oil tanker fleet — 8 Suezmax crude oil tankers

WEBSITE

teekaylng.com/index.aspx?page=home

Section Five

Natural Resources - Coal, Other Minerals, Timber

Alliance Resource Partners

NAME: Alliance Resource Partners, L.P.

STOCK TICKER SYMBOL: NASDAQ: ARLP

ADDRESS

1717 South Boulder Ave
Suite 400
Tulsa, OK 74119

(918) 295-7600

K-1 FORMS: Available online and for Turbo Tax

IPO DATE: August 19, 1999

GENERAL PARTNER

Alliance Holdings GP, L.P.

PRESIDENT, CHIEF EXECUTIVE OFFICER: Joseph W. Craft III

BASIC BUSINESS

Producer and marketer of coal to major United States utilities and industrial users.

Operates 9 underground mining complexes in Illinois, Indiana, Kentucky, Maryland, and West Virginia. Is fifth largest coal producer in eastern U.S.

Current Mining Operations:

1 Pattiki Complex
2 Dotiki Complex
3 Warrior Complex
4 Hopkins Complex
5 Gibson Complex
6 Pontiki Complex
7 MC Mining Complex
8 Mettiki Complex
9 River View Complex

Mines Under Construction:

1. Tunnel Ridge Complex

Mine Development Projects

1. Penn Ridge Complex
2. Gibson South Complex Transfer Terminal
3. Mount Vernon Transfer Terminal

WEBSITE

arlp.com/

Alliance Holdings GP

NAME: Alliance Holdings GP, L.P.

STOCK TICKER SYMBOL: NASDAQ: AHGP

ADDRESS

1717 South Boulder Ave
Suite 400
Tulsa, OK 74119
(918) 295-7600

K-1 FORMS: Available online and for Turbo Tax

IPO DATE: May 15, 2006

GENERAL PARTNER

Alliance GP, LLC

PRESIDENT, CHIEF EXECUTIVE OFFICER: Joseph W. Craft III

BASIC BUSINESS

Is General Partner for Alliance Resource Partners, L.P.

WEBSITE

ahgp.com/

Natural Resource Partners

NAME: Natural Resource Partners, L.P.

STOCK TICKER SYMBOL: NYSE: NRP

ADDRESS

601 Jefferson Street
Suite 3600
Houston, Texas 77002

713-751-7507

K-1 FORMS: Available online and for Turbo Tax

IPO DATE: October 2002

GENERAL PARTNER

NRP GP, LP

Which is a limited partnership. GP Natural Resource Partners LLC is its General Partner and makes decisions for NRP.

It is owned by Robertson Coal Management LLC which is 100% owned by Corbin J. Robertson.

CHIEF EXECUTIVE OFFICER AND CHAIRMAN OF THE BOARD: Corbin J. Robertson, Jr.

BASIC BUSINESS

Coal and aggregates (crushed stone, sand and gravel) production, and coal infrastructure. This includes coal preparations plants, beltlines for transporting coal, coal load-out facilities and other transportation.

In Northern Appalachia, Central Appalachia, Southern Appalachia, Illinois Basin, Northern Powder River Basin, Arizona, Texas, West Virginia and Washington.

Owns 2.1 billion tons of coal reserves.

Subsidiaries: NRP Operating LLC

WEBSITE

nrplp.com/default.aspx

Penn Virginia Resource Partners

NAME: Penn Virginia Resource Partners, L.P.

STOCK TICKER SYMBOL: NYSE: PVR

ADDRESS

100 Matsonford Road
3 Radnor Corporate Center, Suite 300
Radnor, PA 19087

(610) 687-8900
(610) 687-3688 fax

K-1 FORMS: Available online and by Turbo Tax

IPO DATE: 2001

GENERAL PARTNER

Penn Virginia Resource GP, LLC

Which is owned by Penn Virginia GP Holdings, L.P.

Which is owned by Penn Virginia Corporation

CHAIRMAN OF THE BOARD OF DIRECTORS AND CHIEF EXECUTIVE
OFFICER: A. James Dearlove

BASIC BUSINESS

Management of coal and natural resource properties and the gathering and
processing of natural gas.

Owns 829 million tons of proven and probable coal reserves in Central and
Northern Appalachia, the San Juan Basin and the Illinois Basin. Leases out its
mines in return for royalties.

It also owns gas processing plants and gathering systems. PVR Midstream.

And 25% of Thunder Creek Gas Services, LLC ("Thunder Creek"), a joint venture
gathering and transporting coal bed methane in Wyoming's Powder River Basin.

WEBSITE

pvresource.com/

Penn Virginia GP Holdings

NAME: Penn Virginia GP Holdings, L.P.

STOCK TICKER SYMBOL: NYSE: PVG

ADDRESS

100 Matsonford Road
3 Radnor Corporate Center, Suite 300
Radnor, PA 19087

(610) 687-8900
(610) 687-3688 fax

K-1 FORMS: Available online and by Turbo Tax

IPO DATE: June 2006

GENERAL PARTNER

Penn Virginia Corporation

CHAIRMAN OF THE BOARD OF DIRECTORS AND CHIEF EXECUTIVE
OFFICER: A. James Dearlove

BASIC BUSINESS

Is the General Partner for Penn Virginia Resource Partners, L.P.

WEBSITE

pvgpholdings.com/

Pope Resources

NAME: Pope Resources

STOCK TICKER SYMBOL: NASDAQ: POPE

ADDRESS

19245 Tenth Ave. NE
Poulsbo, WA 98370

(360) 697-6626
(360) 697-1156 (fax)

K-1 FORMS: Not available online

IPO DATE: 1985

GENERAL PARTNER

Pope MGP, Inc.

PRESIDENT AND CHIEF EXECUTIVE OFFICER: David L. Nunes

BASIC BUSINESS

Owns land and timber in the Pacific Northwest — 115,000 acres of timberland and 3,000 acres of development property. This is typically raw timber land which POPE helps other developers acquire and prepare for other uses. Also serves as consultant on timberland projects.

114,000 acres owned by POPE and 24,000 owned by funds it has an interest in. Port Gamble WA and Chelais WA. Owns Harbor Hill (Gig Harbor), Wright Creek (Bremerton), Arborwood (Kingston), Port Gamble, and Skamania/Swift Recreation Area.

Subsidiaries: Olympic Resource Management (ORM) and Olympic Property Group (OPG).

WEBSITE

orm.com/default.aspx

Terra Nitrogen Company

NAME: Terra Nitrogen Company, L.P.

STOCK TICKER SYMBOL: NYSE: TNH

ADDRESS

Terra Centre
600 Fourth St
PO Box 6000
Sioux City IA 51102-6000

(712) 277-1340

K-1 FORMS: Available online and by Turbo Tax

IPO DATE: 1990

GENERAL PARTNER

Terra Nitrogen GP, Inc

Which is indirectly owned by Terra Industries, Inc.

PRESIDENT AND CHIEF EXECUTIVE OFFICER: Michael L. Bennett

BASIC BUSINESS

Manufacturer of nitrogen fertilizer products.

Owns one nitrogen manufacturing facility in Verdigris, Oklahoma which manufactures anhydrous ammonia and urea ammonium nitrate solutions (UAN).

Has terminal operations in Blair, Nebraska and Pekin, Illinois.

Operate through Terra Nitrogen Limited Partnership

WEBSITE

terraindustries.com/

Also by Richard Stooker . . .

INCOME INVESTING SECRETS

While the financial markets are collapsing . . .

An Alton Illinois widow and grandmother of two is cashing ever-growing checks, enjoying a secure retirement and living the good life.

Just as she has through every bear market, stock crash and financial fad since 1955 — humiliating the Wall Street pros even though she couldn't analyze a company balance sheet if her life depended on it!

Finally, you too can discover her old-fashioned — yet now revolutionary (and updated for the 21st century) — "gold" egg income investing secrets for lazy investors

Despite following the conventional financial wisdom, many senior citizens are now asking what happened to that worry-free fun and relaxation they promised themselves after a long career of hard work.

Many people in their fifties and early sixties are wondering when — or even if — they'll be able to retire.

What's the alternative? Investing for income.

Learn how to make money whether the stock market goes up, down or sideways.

"Rick Stooker is on the right track. We also intend to pursue a more income-oriented strategy in the years to come. Capital gains are subject to both the risk of a decline in economic fundamentals and a deterioration in market psychology. High-quality dividends and income are subject only to the former, and that makes a big difference in modeling your portfolio returns in retirement."
— *Charles Lewis Sizemore, CFA*
   Senior Analyst, HS Dent Investment Management, LLC

Made in the USA
Lexington, KY
20 September 2010